ALLIED AVIATION OF WORLD WAR I

A PICTORIAL HISTORY OF ALLIED AVIATORS
AND AIRCRAFT OF THE GREAT WAR

AVIATION PIONEERS

ALLIED AVIATION OF WORLD WAR I

A PICTORIAL HISTORY OF ALLIED AVIATORS
AND AIRCRAFT OF THE GREAT WAR

HUGH W. COWIN

First published in Great Britain in 2000 by Osprey Publishing
Elms Court, Chapel Way, Botley, Oxford OX2 9LP, UK
Email: info@ospreypublishing.com

ISBN 1 84176 226 1

Editor: Shaun Barrington
Design: Mark Holt
Origination: Valhaven Ltd, Isleworth, UK
Printed in China through Worldprint Ltd

00 01 02 03 04   10 9 8 7 6 5 4 3 2 1

Other titles in the Aviation Pioneers series:

X-Planes
Research Aircraft 1891–1970
ISBN 185532 876 3

The Risk Takers
Racing and Record Setting Aircraft 1908–1968
ISBN 185532 904 2

German and Austrian Aviation of World War I
ISBN 184176 069 2

Lockheed's Blackworld Skunkworks
U2, SR-71, F117
ISBN 184176 059 5

Acknowledgements

The author is grateful for the unstinted help provided by Andy
Bunce of BAe Systems, John Edwards, Peter Elliott, Gordon Leith
and Simon Moody of the RAF Museum, J.W.'Bill' Himmelreich, Philip
Jarrett, Mike Hooks, Hans Justus Meier, W.E.'Teddy' Nevill of TRH
Pictures and Andrew Siddons of Rolls-Royce. The image source is
indicated with each caption.

FRONT COVER
Top left Caproni Ca 33
Bottom left Nieuport Ni 11 Bebe
Right Captain Edward V. Rickenbacker

REAR COVER
Royal Aircraft Factory RE 8

For a catalogue of all titles published by
Osprey Publishing please contact us at:

Osprey Direct UK
P.O. Box 140, Wellingborough,
Northants NN8 4ZA, UK
E-mail: info@ospreydirect.co.uk

Osprey Direct USA
P.O. Box 130, Sterling Heights,
MI 48311-0130, USA
E-mail: info@ospreydirectusa.com

Or visit our website:
www.ospreypublishing.com

Contents

Preface   6

1 Before the War   8

2 An Aerial Affair   14

3 The Factory's and Other
   People's Efforts   28

4 The Nelson Touch   52

5 Other Allies Contributions   68

6 The Yanks Are Coming!   76

7 1918   86

Index   96

(Frontispiece) Without question the **SE 5a** was the finest design to come from the **Royal Aircraft Factory** during its entire existence. The creation of Henry Folland's fertile mind, the SE 5 series of single seat fighters were both heavier and faster than the Sopwith Camel, which they also preceded into operational service. Despite the long standing claim that the Camel downed more enemy aircraft than its rival, which machine was the best will remain a matter of controversy similar to the Hurricane, versus Spitfire question of the next World War. Certainly, while advocates of the SE 5 have to bow to the Camel's quantative 'kill' superiority, they can point to the generally more pilot friendly handling of the SE 5 and speculate about the Camel's 'kill rate' and on which side of the balance sheet to include all of its own pilots that the unforgiving Camel killed. (Hugh W. Cowin)

Preface

The impact of aviation development on the air war during World War I was profound. Unlike much of the warfare being waged below, the air war was constantly dynamic, not just in the physical sense, but also in terms of its evolution. As the salient points of this evolution in the aircraft and their missions and tactical developments have already been reviewed in the previously published companion volume *German And Austrian Aviation Of World War I*, the writer will confine himself here to a brief resumé. In the initial phase of the war, the role of military aviation was confined to tactical reconnaissance, which was subsequently enhanced in value with the introduction of improved cameras and radio. So effective was the aeroplane as an intelligence gatherer that some form of counter rapidly needed to be found and here the French took the early initiative in developing the fighter as we know it. By late 1915, the early and various attempts to bomb the enemy, often from ill-suited and underpowered aircraft, were beginning to be improved upon by larger, more effective bombers from Russia, Germany and Italy. Similarly during this period, as bigger and better engines were fitted into reconnaissance types increasing their performance, so their role was expanded to include close ground support, or trench strafing. This line of development had by late 1917 led to the emergence of the dedicated armoured close air support machine. Looking at the impact of aviation on warfare in a broader context, these developments taken together had, by mid-1917, led the generals on both sides to demand air superiority over any area they intended to attack.

What is quite fascinating to the author are the areas of marked contrast to be found, beyond the main reconnaissance, fighter and bomber developments common to both both sides, that so show quite different attitudes to air war of the opposing belligerents. Examples of these differing approaches are numerous. As has been stressed in the previous volume, both the Imperial German Army and Navy's immediate pre-war air warfare planning centred around the use of large, rigid airships, both for reconnaissance and bombing. Across the border, it is equally clear that the French spurned this line of development, only maintaining a handful of relatively small, low performance semi-rigid airships by the outbreak of war, these being put to limited use until 1917, when all the Army's airships were transferred to the Navy. In Britain, there was a clear split between the the military, who clearly preferred the aeroplane to the airship for tactical operations, and the Royal Navy, with large expanses of sea to patrol who were more prone to favour the dirigible, albeit of the smaller, semi-rigid variety. Thanks largely to the airship's inherently greater endurance, it lent itself to submarine hunting in what was predominently going to be friendly airspace around the nation's coastline. Later in the war, rather surprisingly in the light of the by then incontrovertible evidence of the large airship's vulnerability, the Royal Navy opted to develop its own series of large airships, albeit by 'piggy-backing' or copying directly German airship technology.

While the author may be critical of the British Admiralty's late support of airship development, he cannot but express admiration for the Royal Navy's pioneering efforts in other areas of air warfare during World War I. Two avenues of development in particular will be dealt with in some depth later in this volume. The prime instance of this was the almost total dominance of naval influence in the development of the British heavy bomber, particularly when their military colleagues were dropping twin engined bomber designs such as the Airco DH 3, in favour of smaller, faster single engined machines, exemplified by the Airco DH 4. The other major area where the Royal Navy's efforts were to impact on the subsequent direction of naval development throughout the world was in mating the new-fangled aeroplane to the warship. Here, the Royal Navy not only soon consolidated the 1911 precedent set by the US Navy of operating an aircraft from a cruiser, they made a huge leap forward by evolving the first of the 'flat-top' aircraft carriers, in the shape of HMS *Furious* and *Argus*.

The success of British heavy bomber development requires some qualification. In fact, Britain's initial deployment of the heavy bomber in the shape of the Handley Page 0/100 was somewhat tardy, not taking place until August 1916. Of the Allied nations, the laurels for the first operational deployment of a heavy bomber must go to the Russians, who were fielding the four-engined Sikorsky Ilya Mourometz as early as February 1915. The second of the Allied countries to use heavy bombers in anger was Italy, whose three-engined Capronis made their debut during late 1915. Significantly, both of these nations flew their first large aircraft in 1913, some time ahead of any comparably sized aircraft flown by the more 'aeronautically developed' nations. Why this was so may have much to do with geography. In the case of Russia, that country's sheer scale virtually predicated that range was going to be one of the first considerations in the mind of any aircraft designer, other than one specializing in fighters. In much more modestly scaled Italy, the problem lay in the country's physical isolation by water and its mountainous northern borders to all but the Balkans. If the Italians were to conduct air strikes against an enemy, then in most sectors of the quadrant, they needed an aircraft with long legs simply to reach its target.

Technologically, the Allies' development of aircraft, whether fighters, bombers or flying boats remained firmly entrenched around wood and bracing wire throughout the war and was thus paced solely by the growth in available engine power. Surprisingly few Allied aircraft designers, or, for that matter, military aircraft procurement agencies showed much interest in such radical developments as light metal structures and the clean, aerodynamically appealing cantilevered monoplane even after the Germans had demonstrated the validity of both during the latter part of the war.

The author apologises in advance for annoying someone, somewhere, by omitting their favourite prototype, the problem, as always, being lack of space. After selecting all of the prominent aircraft types employed, the author has selected from the many minor types those for inclusion here to illustrate some specific point, whether it be a particular technical breakthrough, or more generally their representation of the evolution of the species overall.

In conclusion, one minor but intriguing aspect of the world's first air war: I would draw the reader's attention to something common to the fighter aces of both sides. An inordinately high number of these valiant flyers had initially been rejected by their respective medical authorities as being frail and generally unfit for military service. Maybe, just maybe, this initial rejection was to provide the vital spur to glory.

Below A revealing view depicting the intricacies of stowing and unstowing a **Sopwith Pup** aboard the Royal Navy seaplane carrier, HMS *Manxman*. Remembering that the Pup was among the smallest of naval aircraft, it is understandable that larger machines, such as the Short and Fairey floatplanes that followed, necessarily required wing folding. Incidentally, the Pup seen here, N6454, was one of a 30-aircraft batch built by the Scottish-based William Beardmore. (British Official/Crown Copyright)

Before the War

France had been the first nation to create any form of unified air service, when on 22 October 1910 it brought the previously separate elements of its Army's aviation assets together as the 'Aviation Militaire'. French naval aviation was formally established on 12 March 1912. At the outbreak of war with Germany on 3 August 1914, France, the world's leading proponent of heavier-than-air flying, had the best qualitatively equipped military and naval air arms of all the nations, but was very much in second place to Germany in quantitative terms. However, by way of compensation, France had the largest aeroplane and aero engine manufacturing base extant and was, therefore, in the happy position of not just being able to rapidly gear up to meet its own national needs, but was even able to export significant numbers of aircraft to Britain, whose industrial base was still virtually non-existent. Indeed, between August 1914 and early 1916, both British air services were heavily dependent upon French aircraft builders to fill the gap. There were, however, two main weaknesses in French military aviation compared with that of Germany's at the outset of the war. One of these shortfalls, mentioned above, was the numerical strength of the French air arms, which in the case of the Army comprised 23 squadrons with around 160 aeroplanes, including reserves, plus 12 small airships, along with a vestigial 14 aeroplanes for the Navy. The other weakness and one that was going to take longer to overcome than the numbers shortfall was that of organization. Here, the German Army's aviation units had been grafted into the overall field army structure in such a manner to be far more flexible than the French units, with their unwieldly, overly-centralised command, control and reporting systems. Graphic evidence of this was apparent from the start, with the French military air service taking a two full weeks to mobilise after the initial German thrust onto their soil.

In Britain things progressed a little slower than in France and when the British government of the day got around to consolidating its aviation assets in February 1912, it ruffled the 'top brass' of both Army and Navy by setting up the Royal Flying Corps comprising two wings, one military, the other naval, with a central flying school as the only point of real contact between these fiercely rival services with their different cultures even in terms of aviation. To illustrate this point, the War Office took a formalistic and rigid approach to Army aviation, insisting that in the manner of a previous age, it should control its own aircraft design, development and production through its own Royal Aircraft Factory where possible and only purchase other peoples' aircraft as a matter of last resort. The Royal Navy attitude was far more pragmatic and thus, like their German naval opposite numbers, they bought small numbers of numerous aircraft makes and types that they thought best suited to the task. Intrinsically, this approach brought naval aviators closer to aspirant aircraft manufacturers, such as A.V. Roe, the Short Brothers and 'Tommy' Sopwith than permitted under the Army's system. That the two RFC wings were incompatible had long been apparent, but this became quite clear on 1 July 1914 with the Admiralty's withdrawal of its wing to form the Royal Naval Air Service. Sadly, this ongoing rivalry had already had a generally depressing effect on Britain's embryo aircraft manufacturing base, with the Army producing its own machines in the main, while the Navy distributed what little monies it was given for aviation around too many producers to make anyone rich enough to contemplate expansion. Thus when Britain found itself at war with Germany on 4 August 1914, its total military aeroplane assets numbered less than 200, of which 64 RFC machines, plus 58 RNAS aircraft were deployed to bases in Northwestern France and Belgium over the next few weeks. An even more sobering thought for the war planners to ponder was the minuscule size of Britain's supporting aircraft and aero engine manufacturing base.

Russia's military and naval aviation assets actually surpassed those of Britain in numbers at the beginning of

Below Knights of the air: this evocative image of a pair of two seat **Borel Monoplanes**, plus cavalry, was taken a month or so before the outbreak of World War I. As befitted what was then the world's leading aeronautical nation, the French military air service of the time had mostly monoplanes. The particular machines seen here belonged to the escadrille, or squadron, led by Roger Sommer of pre-war aviation fame, who had learned to fly with Henry Farman in 1909 and who, in the spring of 1910 shared with his erstwhile instructor the honour of making the first night flights by aeroplane. Interestingly, the original note with this picture stated that the aircraft were bomb, as opposed to gun carriers. (Cowin Collection)

August 1914, totalling some 244 aeroplanes and 12 airships, split roughly 70 per cent military and 30 per cent naval. The Russian problem, that had existed since the formal founding of the military air arm on 30 July 1912, was one of overall lack of proper organization, something that was reflected in the sheer variety of types deployed, with all of the attendant supply and maintenance headaches. While Russia's home-based aircraft industry was larger than Britain's at the start of the war it did not remain so. Still, it did manage to produce over 70 examples of the Sikorsky Ilya Moroumetz, the world's first heavy bomber, along with numerous lighter military types, mainly built under licence, prior to Russia's internal collapse and its effective withdrawal from the war in the spring of 1917.

It has been Belgium's bad luck in both World Wars to find itself being used by the German Army as a stepping stone to the coastal ports in the West and Northern France to the South. Not much more than a year after its formation, on 16 April 1913, the still infant Belgium Army Air Corps was to be crushed under the unannounced German invasion of 3 August 1914. At that time the Belgium air arm's order of battle consisted of two squadrons, plus two forming and a fleet of 20 aeroplanes, mainly Farman pushers. What remained of this force joined with French and British forces operating in the Dunkirk to Ostend area. Later in the war, the rebuilt Belgium Air Service was acknowledged for the excellence of its reconnaissance work, while its fighter force, equipped with Hanriot HD-1s, produced no less than three aces with scores in double figures, the most prominent being Willy Coppens with 36 confirmed 'kills'.

Although being almost totally equipped with French aircraft, the Italian military air service has left its indelible mark in the annals of aviation by being the first air arm to fly and fight in anger, when, in late October 1911, a group of Italian pilots flying an assortment of Bleriots and Nieuports carried out armed reconnaissance missions and dropped the first aerial bombs on Turkish troops from their base in Tripoli during the Italo-Turkish War. At the time of the outbreak of war at the beginning of August 1914, Italy was nominally a treaty-bound ally of the Austro-Hungarian Empire, despite the fact that relations were becoming progressively more strained. This detoriation continued to the point where, on 24 May 1915, Italy rescinded the treaty and went to war against the Austro-Hungarians. At this time the country's military aviation inventory consisted of 89 aeroplanes and 3 airships, while the Italian Navy could field 17 aeroplanes, plus 2 airships. If these numbers appear meagre, Italy was at least in the fortunate position of having its own aviation manufactiring base, albeit largely based on producing French aircraft under licence. Within the year this industry was starting to produce home-grown designs, including the first of the very capable Caproni heavy bombers.

The United States of America was the last of the major Allied Powers to join the conflict, doing so on 6 April 1917. Prior to this time naval and military aviation had been somewhat neglected, thanks in no small part to the geographical isolation of the US, coupled to the lack of potentially hostile neighbours with any credible air arm. Of the two services, the US Navy was the first to found a semi-autonomous air service in November 1913, at which time its total stock of aeroplanes was 12. Eight months later, on 18 July 1914, the US Army's aeronautical assets were consolidated as the Aviation Section of the Signal Corps, with 20 aeroplanes on inventory. At the time of America's entry into the war, Army aviation had less than 250 aeroplanes, while the Navy and Marines' combined aeronautical assets consisted of 54 aeroplanes, one small airship and three balloons. At this time the US had an active aircraft industry of its own, but starved of home-based military and naval development funding, was confined to producing training aircraft for the Allies and hence had not enjoyed the colossal rates of growth enjoyed by its European rivals.

Below The creation of Geoffrey de Havilland, the two-seat **Royal Aircraft Factory BE 2** made its debut in the late spring of 1912 and was essentially a slightly uprated engined development of the previous years one-off BE 1. Unlike the BE 1, however, the original BE 2 was not just to establish a new British altitude record for two-seaters in June 1912, when de Havilland and his passenger reached 10,560 feet, but was to prove to be a true survivor – some would argue it survived too long – in the process siring a family of BE 2 production variants that would account for a further 3,241 aircraft. Seen here is BE 2a, serial no. 206, photographed wearing an experimental oleo landing gear, along with streamlined cuffs at the upper end of its interplane struts. As with all 14 BE 2as, this machine was powered by a 70hp Renault, which gave it a top level speed of 70mph at sea level, falling to 65mph at 6,500 feet. (RAE/Crown Copyright)

Above right The 1912-built **Bayard 'Fleurus'** airship was powered by a 150hp engine, driving twin propellers to give it a top level speed of 36mph. Based at Verdun when the war started, 'Fleurus' is claimed to have made the first Allied sortie over Germany, on the night of 9-10 August 1914, dropping bombs on the town of Trier. At this time the French Army's inventory of operational airships totalled just four, all non-rigid and far inferior in performance and range to their larger German contemporaries from Schutte-Lanz and Zeppelin. (Cowin Collection)

Below Thanks to its 71mph top level speed at sea level and 13,100 feet operating ceiling, both of which were superior to most contempoary two-seaters, the 80hp Gnome-powered **Morane-Saulnier Type L** had already been acquired in small numbers by the French military prior to the war. First flown during the earlier half of 1913, the Type L made an admirable reconnaissance machine at the outset of hostilities and was subsequently adopted as an armed fighting scout. In fact there were two versions of the Type L, the earlier one, seen here, using wing warping, while the later Type LA employed ailerons. Both versions served with the French, but the LA, which was built in far greater numbers, was also flown by the British and Russians. In all, around 635 examples were to be produced. (Cowin Collection)

Below The single seat **Morane-Saulnier Type M** made its first appearance during the late summer of 1912 in civilian guise aimed at the sports and racing enthusiast. Powered by a 80 hp

Gnome, the Type M had a top level speed of 78mph and was soon offered in modified armoured form to the military as a fast, unarmed scout. While the French appear not to have acquired the Type M, the British War Ministry are reported to have bought three, while the machine seen here, serial no. 5707, was one of 25 ordered by the British Admiralty. The purchase was subsequently cancelled. (Cowin Collection)

Above The remarkably clean, almost visionary **Royal Aircraft Factory BS 1** was another creation of designer/pilot Geoffrey de Havilland and made its debut in early 1913. Extolled by the noted early military aviation historian, J.M.Bruce, as being the sire of all future single seat fighters of World War I, the BS 1 had what can only be described as a vivid performance, for its day, being capable of 92mph, coupled to a 900 feet per minute initial rate of climb. All this on the power of an 80hp Gnome! In its earliest form, seen here, the BS 1's rudder, unaided by any fin, was simply inadequate to provide effective directional control and anyway was too weak, as it demonstrated by breaking away on 27 March 1913, breaking de Havilland's jaw in the ensuing crash. Rebuilt with a more effective tail unit, the aircraft became the **SE 2**. (Cowin Collection)

Below A young 'Tommy', later **Sir Thomas Octave Murdoch Sopwith**, seen here with his wife, sitting at the controls of one of his early machines, a Howard Wright biplane, during the Sopwiths' May to October 1911 visit to the US. Independently wealthy, 'Tommy' was born on 18 January 1888 and had been given a grounding in engineering as part of his education. At university 'Tommy' mixed with people such as the Hon. Charles Rolls of later Rolls-Royce fame, companions who had shown him the lure of motoring, power boating and ballooning. 'Tommy' made his first balloon ascent in 1907. On 22 October 1910, he bought a Howard Wright monoplane and having been given two brief accompanied demonstration flights felt sufficiently confident to tackle a solo flight. This and many other early flights terminated in a crash, but despite these upsets 'Tommy' gained Aero Club Aviator's Certificate No 31 on 21 November 1910. Less than a month later 'Tommy', flying his Howard Wright biplane, beat six competitors to win the prestigious Baron de Forest prize worth £4,000 by covering a straight line distance of 169 miles from Eastchurch in Kent to Beaumont in southern Belgium – a British record that was to stand for four years. Following his highly successful 1911 US tour as an exhibition pilot, he set up the Sopwith School of Flying at Brooklands in early 1912. Here, he taught a number of pupils to fly who would later come to fame, including Hugh 'Boom' Trenchard, held by many to be the father of the RAF and an Australian named H. G. 'Harry' Hawker, of whom more will be said later. On 8 June 1912, 'Tommy' was to win the first ever Aerial Derby, flying his 70hp Bleriot XI to reach an average of 58.5mph. At the end of 1912, he formed the Sopwith Aviation Company, from which so many famous British combat aircraft were to flow. On the back of these efforts that produced the Pup, Triplane, Camel and Snipe, 'Tommy' went on to build the huge Hawker Siddeley industrial empire, embracing far more than aircraft alone. Sir Thomas died at the age of 101, on 27 January 1989. (Cowin Collection)

Above The **Sopwith Three Seater** of 1913 was an impressive performer, with the power of its 80hp Gnome setting a number of British altitude records in June and July 1913, in the hands of the by then Sopwith Chief Test Pilot, 'Harry' Hawker. Of these the highest reached was 12,900 feet with one passenger. The Three Seater could carry a 450lb payload at 70mph. At least seven of these machines were known to have been operated by the naval wing of the RFC. (Cowin Collection)

Below Three of these 100hp **Anzani** powered, two-seater **Sopwith seaplanes**, serial nos 58 to 60, were built for the Admiralty in 1913, the first being delivered in July of that year. Photographic evidence exists to show that No 58 was flown as a landplane by the RNAS Eastchurch contingent sent to France in the early weeks of the war. No information appears to have survived about the machines' performance. (Cowin Collection)

Right **Edwin Alliot Verdon Roe**, seen here standing beside his Roe III two-seat triplane of 1910, was born near Manchester on 26 April 1877. 'A.V.' Showed an early aptitude for the more technical subjects, cemented by serving a five year apprentice-ship at a railway works between 1893 and 1898. Next, 'A.V.' turned to things maritime, hoping to join the Royal Navy, but ending up by spending four years in the merchant marine. It was while at sea that 'A.V.' started to study bird flight, which by 1902 had led him into aeromodelling. 'A.V.'s success in this field got him the post of Secretary to the Aero Club in the spring of 1906, but the lure of joining an American project to build a steam-powered vertical take-off and landing aircraft proved too much and in a matter of weeks 'A.V.' had set off for Denver, Colorado. 'A.V.' Returned to Britain in the autumn of 1906, following the collapse of the project and by January 1907 had embarked on the design of his own first full-size, man-carrying aircraft, the 6hp JAP-powered Roe I canard biplane. Once re-engined with the more manful 25hp Antoinette, this machine, piloted by 'A.V.', made what was arguably the first flight by a British Aircraft on 8 June 1908. Just over a year later 'A.V.' Gained Aero Club Aviator's Certificate No 18, flying his Roe III triplane. During the whole of this period, from 1906 to 1910, 'A.V.' was living in near poverty. In 1910, with help from his family, 'A.V.' Founded A.V. Roe and Company and in July 1911 gave up flying to concentrate on the design work that was to establish him as one of the country's leading aircraft designers, with such machines as his Avro 504. 'A.V.' sold his interest in Avro in 1928 and received his knighthood the following year, during which he bought a controlling interest in what was, ther-after, to be Saunders Roe, of which he remained President until his death on 4 January 1958. (Cowin Collection)

Above Powered by a 100hp Gnome, the **Avro Type H**, or **503**, derived from the Avro 501 floatplane and made its first flight on 28 May 1913. Ironically this particular machine was bought by the German Navy and is seen undergoing their acceptance trials at Worthing, Sussex in June 1913. An additional three examples were built, all for the British Admiralty. Top level speed of this two-seater floatplane was 64mph at sea level. Incidentally, many of the Type H's features were to find their way into the later Gotha WD-I, shown on page 29 of *German and Austrian Aviation of World War I*. (Cowin Collection)

Top right The founder of a dynasty, the original **Avro 504**. Powered by an 80hp Gnome rotary, this machine made its first flight in July 1913, piloted by F .P. 'Fred' Raynham. Destined to carve itself a prominent place in the annals of aviation, the redoubtable Avro 504 first served as both a bomber and a fighter during the first year of war, prior to being selected to serve as the RAF's standard basic training machine for most of the next two decades. The first military interest in the 504 manifested itself in a War Office order for twelve RFC machines, placed in the summer of 1913. No further orders were received until after the outbreak of war. The 504's top level speed was 82mph (Avro)

Below Fifteen months or so after the **Royal Aircraft Factory** had produced the breathtaking BS I, they once again broke the mould with their extremely advanced **SE 4** scout, which made its debut in June 1914. The machine is seen here in August 1914, shortly after being fitted with more conventional landing gear than the unsatisfactory original item. This one-off single seater, serial no 628, used a neatly cowled 160hp twin row Gnome rotary, giving it an astonishing top level speed of 135mph at sea level, along with an equally impressive 1,600 feet per minute initial rate of climb. Regrettably, the sole SE 4 was damaged beyond repair in a landing accident on 12 August 1914. Even more tragically, this mishap appears to have deterred any further development of the type. (RAE/Crown Copyright)

Below The sole side-by-side two seat **Sopwith Trainer**, serial no 149 of 1914, reputedly built specifically for the young, air-minded First Lord of the Admiralty, Winston S. Churchill. Powered by an 80hp Gnome, later replaced by a 100hp rotary of the same make, this aircraft has been referred to in various Sopwith records as being both the **Sociable** and the **Churchill**. (Cowin Collection)

An Aerial Affair

Part of the diplomatic niceties that were consolidated in the Renaissance period (but had been around for many centuries before) was a desire for national governments to be seen to behave in a civilised manner. This meant that even if some mighty aggressor launched an unannounced assault on a neighbour's territory, it should, simultaneously, pronounce that a state of war existed and, if possible, include an allusion to some alleged misbehaviour on the part of the other nation, by way of justifying its own action. In the case of Germany's 3 August 1914 declaration of war against France, mention was made of French aerial infringements of German airspace as being a contributory factor.

In the month or so of relatively mobile warfare that followed the initial German assault, the limitations of French reconnaissance aircraft and more particularly their post-flight reporting system frequently rendered their efforts next to useless, but as reporting and tactical analysis systems improved, so the value of the fliers' efforts increased. Indeed, it was aerial reconnaissance of German troop movements between 1 and 4 September 1914 that enabled the French to successfully counter a major German thrust aimed at taking Paris. The military aircraft was beginning to justify itself.

What followed during the latter months of 1914 was a simultaneous effort to expand the rate of aircraft production, which was successful, and the introduction of organizational changes aimed at improving operational efficiency. This latter effort proved only partially successful, with perhaps too early an emphasis on building up a bombing force at the expense of reconnaissance assets. In fairness, however, it should be pointed out that up to this time, only a handful of aircraft had been brought down by enemy action on either side of the lines, which may have bolstered the confidence of the bombing proponents.

1915 started off with little change in terms of overall air activity, but behind the scenes, France was expending much effort on the development of a more effective fighter than the machine gun-equipped pusher-engined machines that had a marvellous field of forward fire, but, thanks to their lack of speed, were all too frequently hard pressed to catch up on their would-be prey. Paul Saulnier of Morane-Saulnier fame had been working on an interrupter gear that would permit a machine gun to fire through the propeller arc without shooting off the blades for some months, but was being constantly stymied by the sensitivity of the mechanism to variations in the rounds of ammunition being fed to the gun. Tasked with solving the problem, the noted pre-war French aviator, Roland Garros, along with his mechanic, took a cruder approach, talked to Panard, who knew something about armour cladding, and came up with the armoured propeller cuff that simply deflected any bullet hitting it. This is just what military aviators everywhere had been waiting for, as it allowed the fitting of a fixed, forward-firing gun aimed by the pilot, who simply flew his whole aircraft at the enemy, firing when within range. The armoured cuff allowed the use of fast, single seaters

in place of the slower two-man gun carriers. The classic single-seat fighter had been born. By the early summer of 1915, French fighter forces, equipped with Morane-Saulnier Type L and Ns were exacting a heavy toll on German reconnaissance aircraft.. However, as is always the case, this temporary French aerial supremacy was not to last for long, with Immelmann and Boelcke receiving their own interrupter gear-equipped Fokker Eindekkers in the late summer, thus beginning the era of the 'Fokker Scourge'. What was very noticeable in this early air fighting was the relative rarity of single fighter-on-fighter combat, the fighter pilots of both sides tending to concentrate on two-seater 'kills'.

The first four months of 1916 brought a continuation in German air fighting superiority they had held from the end of 1915, when the Germans had introduced new tactics that further stretched French fighter resources. Things were to shift again in favour of the French when, in the spring of 1916, Commandant Tricornot de Rose, Chief of the French 2nd Army's Aviation Corps, gathered eight of the 15 existing French fighter squadrons outside Behonne, near the besieged ring of fortresses surrounding Verdun. This tactic, combined with the introduction of the fast, agile Nieuport 11 Bebe, may have neutralised the previous German ascendancy, but the potential was rather dissipated by the French fighter pilots' reluctance to fight in packs; a tactic that would later be taken up successfully first by the Germans and then later by the British.

Meanwhile, the products of the priority French bomber building programme, mainly in the shape of various Voisin or Farman variations on the pusher-engined theme were proving incapable of carrying a sensible bomb load over more than a few miles, while their lack of performance made them easy prey to German fighters. From this point on, until the debut of the fast Breguet 14 in late 1917, French bombing operations became progressively more limited, with many of the bombers being shifted to reconnaissance duties. What long range bombing that did take place tended to be done by lone French bomber crews, whose bravery, sadly, far outstripped their effectiveness. Surprisingly, in the light of the effectiveness of the German long-range bombing attacks of 1917 on both London and Paris, the French largely neglected heavy bomber development to the point where they were compelled to operate Italian-designed Caproni Ca 45s, pending the arrival of the Farman F60 Goliath, whose 1918 debut was far too late to impact on events.

Sad to relate for a nation that had entered the war as the unassailable world leader in aeronautics, France appears to have spent its war going backwards in terms of aviation technology. Touching upon this topic in the preface to *X-Planes*, the first in the *Aviation Pioneers* series, the author pointed out that combat aircraft devel-opment in both world wars was largely confined to building bigger, more powerful next-generation variations on an existing theme, as was certainly the case with French aircraft development during World War I. While minor miracles may have taken place with regards to the

increase in production between 1915 and 1918, little of an aerodynamic or structural material advance is evident when comparing examples of France's finest, such as the 1915 Nieuport 11, to either the SPAD XIII or even later Nieuports 28 and 29, albeit the later machines were far more robust and powerful.

Above Three French operated two seat **Nieuport 12s** joining the airfield's left-handed traffic pattern above another group of Ni 12s in the foreground. The solitary Nieuport 17 on the ground near the centre of the picture points to the photograph being taken some time after February 1916. (Cowin Collection)

Below The **Bleriot Type XI-2 Artillerie**, as its name implies, was employed on reconnaissance for the artillery and entered service with the French and Italians during 1911. At the outbreak of war, this 70hp Gnome-engined two seater was in service with the French, Britain's RFC and RNAS, Belgium and Italy. Its relatively meagre top level speed of 66mph at sea level was no great problem at a time when effective anti-aircraft artillery or fighters were yet to make an appearance, while its 3.5 hour endurance provided a useful time aloft. (Cowin Collection)

Above Typically powered by a 160hp Renault, the two-seat **Farman F 40** series of pusher-engined reconnaissance bombers were built in considerable numbers during 1915, eventually going into service with almost fifty French squadrons, as well as serving with the RNAS, who had 50, the Belgians and Russians. Top level speed depended upon the engine installed, but the Renault-powered F 56 version, seen here having fallen into German hands, could reach 82mph at 6,560 feet. (Cowin Collection)

Below The two seat **Farman HF 22** derived from the pre-war Farman F 16 and when fielded in 1914 as a reconnaissance bomber proved somewhat underpowered under the urging of its 80hp Gnome. Hampered by its limited top speed of 65mph at sea level, the HF 22 took a severe mauling from the enemy and by mid-1915 had been withdrawn from front-line duties to the training role. The type served with the French, both British service arms and Belgium. (Cowin Collection)

Opposite, top Initially deployed as a reconnaissance type in late 1914, the two-seat **Caudron G III's** lack of speed and effective defence soon saw its withdrawal from front-line use in other than the Balkan and Russian theatres of operation. However, as with the Avro 504, the G III was to make its mark as a trainer, where it served with the French, both the RFC and RNAS, plus the US Army Air Service. Fitted with various engines in the 80hp to 100hp range, the twin 80hp Le Rhone powered French machine, seen here, had a top speed of 82mph at 6,560 feet, a ceiling of 14,000 feet and could stay aloft for up to 4 hours. (Cowin Collection)

learning to fly prior to the war. He joined the military aviation service in September 1914, his first operational unit being MF 8, flying Maurice Farmans. Unhappy with his lot, Navarre kept pestering his superiors for a transfer to fighters, succeeding in his aim early in 1915, when he went to MS 12. On the strength of the above mentioned 'kill', Navarre was promoted from corporal to sergeant and given a single-seat Morane-Saulnier Type N. By early 1916 Navarre had been promoted to Sub Lieutenant, joining Escadrille N 67 that was flying the Nieuport 11 Bebe. Navarre, both impulsive and impetuous by nature, had the fuselage of his machine, serial no N872, painted an attention-grabbing scarlet. Fond of flying up close to his prey to ensure his fire would have maximum effect, this tactic was to prove his undoing when, on 17 June 1916, he was downed with a severe head wound from an observer's bullet. Hospitalised for around two years, Navarre was reluctantly allowed to return to flying, only to kill himself on 10 July 1919, while practicing to fly through the Arc de Triomphe. As one of the early French fighter pilots, Navarre had left the scene too early to have amassed more than 12 confirmed victories. (Cowin Collection)

Below **Jean Marie Dominique Navarre**, seen here as a sergeant pilot serving with Escadrille MS 12 towards the close of 1915. The machine he is standing before is a Morane-Saulnier Type L of the kind in which he and his observer scored his first victory, when they downed a two-seat Aviatik on 1 April 1915. This was within a few hours of Roland Garros having bagged his first 'kill' and at a time when downing an enemy aircraft was still a very rare event. Born in 1895, Jean Navarre had started

one Hotchkiss or one Lewis gun was mounted forward. Built in quantity, the Type III was used by France, Belgium, Russia and Britain's RNAS, an example of which is seen here, operating from the northeastern Aegean island of Imbros during the early summer of 1915. (British Official/Crown Copyright)

Opposite, top **Charles Eugene Jules Marie Nungesser** ended his war with 45 confirmed victories, placing him in third place among France's leading air aces. Seen here leaning against his Nieuport 23, serial no N1895, resplendent with his macabre personal emblem, Nungesser was born in Paris on 15 March 1892. Clearly both impetuous and self-confident, the young Nungesser had run off to Argentina at the age of 16, where he made his first flight, 'soloing' the machine immediately afterwards. Commissioned as a cavalry officer into the 2nd Hussars prior to the war, Nungesser found himself overtaken by the advancing German in August 1914, coolly extricating himself by ambushing an enemy staff car, shooting its two occupants, and using it to make his escape. For this feat, along with an earlier act of bravery, Nungesser received the Medaille Militaire, along with a transfer to the flying service. On 8 April 1915 and by now a qualified pilot, he joined Escadrille VB 106, flying two-seat Voisins. It was while flying one of these sedate pushers in the autumn of 1915 that he was to make his first 'kill' by downing an Albatros two seater. Clearly, this victory marked him as being fighter pilot material, his tranfer to Escadrille N 65, with its single seat Nieuport 11s following in November 1915. Once with N 65, Nungesser displayed an impressive aggression, as reflected in his ever-mounting tally of 'kills'. Reckless to the point of foolhardiness, helped, no doubt, by the military publicists, Charles Nungesser was feted wherever he went despite the fact that he spent much time in hospital recovering not only from enemy-inflicted wounds, but car crashes of his own making. Nungesser was to survive the war, his legend following him to the end, when, on 8 May 1927, accompanied by Francois Coli in the Levasseur 'Oiseau Blanc', he took off in an attempt to make the first east-west Atlantic crossing by aeroplane. Neither the aircraft or its crew were ever seen again. (Cowin Collection)

Above The shoulder-winged **Morane-Saulnier Type N** single seater had been completed early in 1914 and was actually in Austria being demonstrated by Roland Garros to the authorities there on 28 June 1914, the day Prince Franz Ferdinand was assassinated and set in train the events quickly leading to war in Europe. Early examples of the Type N that went into French service in 1914 were powered with the 80hp Gnome, as were a small batch delivered to the Imperial Russian Air Service, whereas the final machines delivered to the RFC used the 110hp Le Rhone. Top level speed was 102mph at 6,560 feet, while the aircraft's operational ceiling was 13,125 feet. During the spring of 1915, the Type N, previously used as a fast, unarmed scout, was fitted with the Garros-devised bullet deflecting propeller cuffs and a Hotchkiss machine gun and transformed into a fighter, as with the French machine seen here. Not built in great numbers, the French took only 49 to equip Escadrille MS 23, while the Russians formed one squadron and the RFC took sufficient to partially equip Nos 3 and 60 squadrons. (Cowin Collection)

Below The series of Voisin pusher-engined, two seaters initially entered service with the French prior to the war and through improvments continued to flow into service through to early 1918. The **Voisin LA, or Type III**, depicted here, entered service in early 1915 and used a 130hp Salmson-built Canton-Unne 9M. The Type III's top level speed was a modest 76mph at 6,560 feet. The machine carried a 460lb bombload over a range of 250 miles at a cruising speed of 59mph. By way of defence

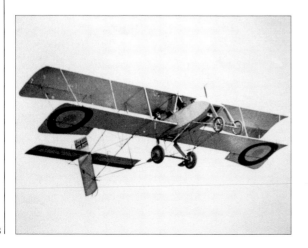

Above The 150hp Salmson-built Canton-Unne powered **Voisin LB, or Type 4**, two seater, that made its operational debut in early 1916 was one of the first dedicated ground attack machines. Armed with either a 37mm cannon, as seen here, or an even larger 47mm weapon, the Type 4 proved equally effective against railway trains or shipping and was operated by both the French military and naval air arms, plus the Italians. (Cowin Collection)

Left **Georges Marie Ludovick Jules Guynemer** is seen here briefing General Franchet d'Espery on the finer point of the SPAD VII's Hispano-Suiza engine in June 1917. Like the German fighter ace, Theo Osterkamp, Guynemer was initially rejected for military service on the grounds of his weak physique. Born in Paris on 24 December 1894, Guynemer befriended the local airfield commandant in order to enlist as an aircraft mechanic on 24 November 1914. Once in the service and with a little help from his well-placed father's contacts, Guynemer had been selected for pilot training by March 1915. As a corporal pilot, Georges joined Escadrille MS 3, flying a mix of single and two seat Morane-Saulniers. Initially given a two seater Type L, Guynemer scored an early victory, when he and his observer downed a two seat Aviatik during July 1915. By the end of 1915 Guynemer's unit was flying Nieuport 11s, becoming N 3 in the process. His score now stood at three. Commissioned in February 1916, Guynemer was wounded and missed most of the intensive air fighting over the Verdun area during the first half of 1916. Recovered, Georges rejoined N 3 just in time to take part in the Battle of the Somme, that opened on 1 July 1916. Guynemer experienced mixed luck on 23 September 1916, when, after downing three enemy aircraft, he, himself, narrowly missed death when his SPAD VII was shot out of the sky by 'friendly fire'. The culprit on this occassion was a 75mm French anti-aircraft shell that hit his machine at 9,000 feet. George was lucky to be able to get his fighter down for a crash landing. Sadly, luck finally deserted Guynemer on 11 September 1917, when the Legion d'Honneur holding ace was surprised by a flight of Albatros fighter and fell to their guns. At this time, Georges Guynemer had scored 45 confirmed victories. (Cowin Collection)

Above The spritely little **Nieuport 11 Bebe** single seater had been designed during the summer of 1914 to compete in that year's James Gordon Bennett air race, an event that was, sadly, overtaken by the war. Happily, however, the military were impressed by the Bebe's speed and agility, with, in chronological order of purchase, the Governments of Britain, France, Belgium, Italy and Russia buying it for use as a fast, unarmed scout. Initially ordered in relatively small numbers, the Bebe's sales prospects went sky high when in the summer of 1915, this brainchild of Gustav Delage was to make its debut fitted with an overwing .303 inch Lewis gun that fired forward and above the propeller arc. This may have meant the pilot was temporarily distracted by having to swing the gun backwards and down through an arc each time he needed to reload, but this was far outweighed by the benefit of a higher 'burst' rate of fire, unimpeded as the weapon was by interrupter or synchronising gear. Powered by an 80hp Le Rhone, the Bebes had a top level speed of 97mph at sea level, along with an impressive rate of climb and a 15,000 feet ceiling. When the Bebe became operational towards the close of 1915, it, along with the Airco DH 2, were soon to turn the air superiority tide in favour of the Allies, with the Bebe, in particular, proving more than a match for the previously dreaded Fokker Eindekker. This said, the machine did have a pitfall and a potentially fatal one at that in the guise of its 'V' interplane strut and its lower mainplane pick-up. If overstressed, this weak element could cause shedding of the lower wing, which in parting with the rest of the airframe frequently and unsurprisingly caused a progressive failure of the machine's overall structure and the inevitable loss of the pilot's life. Bebe

pilots therefore needed to learn not to wrestle the controls too hard at high speed, or pay the ultimate penalty. (Cowin Collection)

Below The **Morane-Saulnier Type P** two seat reconnaissance machine was a derivative of the their Type LA. Initially deployed operationally in mid-1916, the Type P was produced with a choice of 80hp Le Rhone, with the French military designation Type XXI, or with a 110hp Le Rhone, when it became the Type XXVI. Seen here is a French operated Type XXVI that had a top level speed of 97mph at 6,560 feet, along with a ceiling of 12,000 feet. Armament comprised a fixed, forward firing gun for the pilot, together with a flexibly mounted gun for the observer. Operated in some numbers by the French military, a much smaller quantity were operated by RFC squadrons well into 1917, with at least 565 Type Ps known to have been produced. (Cowin Collection)

Below The **Nieuport 16** proved to be an only partially successful attempt to extend the production life of the Ni 11 Bebe. To do this, the company replaced the Bebe's 80hp rotary with the bigger and heavier 110hp Le Rhone making the machine notoriously nose heavy, particularly with power off. Most Ni 16s ended their days by having their gun removed and replaced by eight Le Prieur rockets for use as 'Zeppelin chasers', as in the case of this French machine. (*Cowin Collection*)

Below Powered by a pusher-mounted 220hp Renault, the two seat **Breguet-Michelin BM IV** bomber entered service in early 1916, but compared with the standard Voisins was more prone to spin as well as offering the pilot poorer lateral visibility. Capable of carrying up to forty 16lb bombs on its two underwing racks, visible here just outboard of the main wheels, the BM IV had a top level speed of 84mph at sea level. 100 of these machines were presented to France by the Michelin Brothers, with another 25 built for the RNAS under licence by Graham White as their Type 19. This French-operated aircraft, seen here behind the German lines, had been forced down during the autumn of 1916. (*Cowin Collection*)

Above right The **Salmson-Moineau** three seater of early 1916 was an extremely novel, well armed if clearly underpowered reconnaissance type. Initially powered by a 120hp Canton-Unne mounted behind the nose gunner's position, this engine drove twin tractor-mounted propellers set midway up the

inboard interplane struts via transmission shafting. Even when later re-engined to take the 240hp Salmson engine, as seen here, the machine's top level speed was only 80.9mph. Just visible in this image are the paired guns, flexibly mounted in both nose and rear cockpits. (*Cowin Collection*)

Below The French, who until now had been a prime supplier of aircraft to both the RFC and RNAS, saw the RFC using the **Sopwith 1½ Strutter** as two-seat fighters to good effect during the July 1916 Battle of the Somme and were impressed enough to promptly negotiate a licence to build the aircraft and put it into large scale production. Indeed, of the total 5,720 examples built, 4,200 were French-produced. Why this was so has much to do with the palpable failure of France's own earlier bomber programme touched on at the start of this chapter. As it was, the French chose to produce the 1½ Strutter in both single-seat bomber and two-seat reconnaissance form, but ran into delivery problems, as a result of which the mass of French aircraft were not delivered until the summer of 1918, by which time they were obsolescent, if not obsolete. As a two seater, the machine was usually powered by a 110hp Clerget that gave a top level speed of 106mph at sea level, along with a ceiling of 15,000 feet. In comparision, the single-seat bombers, with their various 110hp or 130hp rotaries could carry a bomb load of up to 224lb and had a top level speed of 102mph at 6,560 feet. Of the French machines, 514 were purchased by the American Expeditionary Force, while the type also served in small numbers with the air arms of Belgium, Latvia, Romania and Russia. Note the distinctive camouflage scheme applied to this French-built and operated example. (*Cowin Collection*)

Left **Rene Pierre Marie Dorme** joined the French Army in 1913, subsequently serving with an artillery unit in Northern Africa. Born on 30 January 1894, Dorme transferred to the flying service in early 1915, passing out as a pilot on 6 May 1915. For a little over a year, between 5 June 1915 to 25 June 1916, Dorme flew reconnaissance in two-seat Caudrons with Escadrille C 94 , prior to joining the single-seat Nieuport 17-equipped Escadrille N 3, soon to become SPA 3 with SPAD VIIs. Dorme's first confirmed 'kill' came when he downed an LVG two seater on 9 July 1916. By 20 December 1916, when Dorme was severely wounded, his 'kill' score had risen to 17. Commissioned as a sub lieutenant during his convalescence. Dorme returned to his unit on 1 March 1917. Less than three months later Dorme was killed in combat, on 25 May 1917, at which time his confirmed victories totalled 23. (Cowin Collection)

Below and bottom The **Nieuport 17** went into operational service in the late spring of 1916 being a bigger, better, more powerful development of the Nieuport 11 Bebe, minus the handling problems of the Ni 16. Powered by a 110hp Le Rhone, the Ni 17 had a top level speed of 107mph at 6,560 feet giving

it a level speed advantage of around 13mph over the Halberstadt D II and 16mph compared with the Fokker E III. This, combined with its superior climb and agility saw the new French fighter outclassing its German opposition to the point where the German reaction was to have Euler and Siemens-Schuckert mimic the design by 'back-engineering' a captured Nieuport 17. The early production French-operated example seen here sported a 'cone de pénétration', which, unlike a normal airscrew boss, remained stationary. However, like many adornments dreamt up by the aircraft builders, these cones failed to survive long in operational use, as shown by this ground view of late production Nieuport 17, serial no N1559. With these later machines the overwing Lewis gun was replaced by a synchronised .303 inch Vickers firing through the propeller arc. N1559 is in standard French markings. The fact that the machine is fitted with a totally non-standard pitot/static tube, fitted to the portside 'V' interplane strut, would indicate that N1559 was involved in development flying. Despite the high speed manoeuvre limitations of the earlier Bebe also applying to the Ni 17, the fighter was built in quantities that approached the 1,000 aircraft mark, the type entering widespread service in France, with both the RFC and RNAS in Britain, Belgium, Italy – where 150 were licence-built by Macchi – The Netherlands and Romania. (Cowin Collection)

Below First flown in the spring of 1915, the two-man, twin 80hp Le Rhone-powered **Caudron G IV** was an attempt to remedy the operational shortfalls of the company's G III, without, it must be said, much success. Carrying a fairly meagre 250lb bomb load and with a top level speed of 82mph at 6,560 feet, the G IV proved almost as vulnerable in combat as its single-engined predessor. The G IV went became operational in late 1915, serving with French, RNAS and Italian squadrons, the machine being withdrawn from front-line use during the autumn of 1916. (Cowin Collection)

Above Externally almost identical to the later Nieuport 17s, the **Nieuport 23** was fitted with a 120hp Le Rhone and carried its Vickers gun on the port, or lefthand side of the upper nose, rather than the top centre as on late model 17s. Top level speed of the Ni 23 was 115mph at sea level. The machine shown here, N1895, was the personal mount of French ace, Charles Nungesser. (Cowin Collection)

Below Although somewhat uglier in appearance, the two-seat **Dorand AR I** reconnaissance type of mid-1916 bore an uncanny configurational resemblance to its near contemporary Bristol F2A. Top level speed of the Dorand was 93.2mph at 4,920 feet, considerably less than that of the F2A, despite the Dorand's 200hp Renault producing 10hp more than the F2A's Rolls-Royce Falcon. The AR I entered limited operational use as an artillery spotter in April 1917. Its .303-inch armament consisted of a fixed, forward-firing Vickers for the pilot, coupled with either one or two flexibly mounted Lewis guns in the rear cockpit. (Cowin Collection)

Below and inset Big, brutal and heavy, the **SPAD S VII** was the aircraft destined to usurp the Nieuport 17 as France's leading fighter. First flown in May 1916, the S VII initially employed a water-cooled 140hp Hispano-Suiza, whose output was progressively coaxed to give 150hp, then 160hp and, ultimately, 175hp, giving the later S VIIs a top level speed of 119mph at 6,560 feet. Although lacking the Nieuport 17's agility, the S VII more than made up this shortfall by virtue of its higher speed and really robust structure, the latter advantage gaining more importance in people's minds coming as it did at a time when the structural weakness of the Nieuport's wings was beginning to create genuine anxiety. The S VII's armament consisted of a .303-inch Vickers gun synchronised to fire through the

propeller arc. Deliveries of the S VII with 150hp engine started in early September 1916, the type going to both the French and RFC squadrons. Of these early S VIIs, some 495 were French-built, while a further 200 were produced under licence in Britain. These were followed by around 6,000 of the improved S VIIbis with the 175hp engine, the S VII eventually serving with many air arms, including those of Belgium, Brazil, Greece, Italy, Peru, Portugal, Romania, Russia and the US expeditionary force. The stork emblem on the S VII seen here identifies it as belonging the the famed Group de Chasse 12 commanded by Felix Brocard. The inset shows an S VII of Escadrille SPA 31 that had been forced down behind enemy lines and carries the legend 'Acquired by Jasta 38, 6 April 1917' in German just aft and below the cockpit coaming. (*Cowin Collection*)

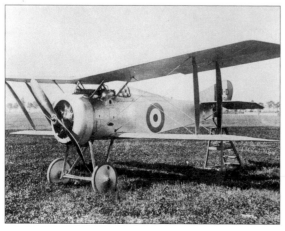

Left The **Hanriot HD-1** made its debut towards the close of 1916 and although never built in anything like the numbers enjoyed by the Nieuport 17 or SPAD S VII, displayed a robustness that belied its rather frail appearance. Initially deployed operationally during the summer of 1917 and much beloved by those that flew it, the HD-1 was largely overlooked in the land of its origin, with only the French Navy buying 35. Outside its homeland, this typically 120hp Le Rhone-powered single seater found favour with the Belgian and Italian air arms. Belgium took 125, while Italy acquired no less than 831 HD-1s, which they preferred to the SPAD XIII. The only real criticism of the HD-1 appears to have been of its single .303-inch synchronised Vickers gun armament, generally considered to lack much 'clout' by mid-1917. Unfortunately, attempts to add a second gun seriously affected the machine's climb and altitude performance. (*Cowin Collection*)

Left **Rene Paul Fonck** was born in the Alsace province of France on 27 March 1894 and entered the Army as an enlisted man at the outbreak of hostilities. In February 1915, Fonck transferred to the flying service, where he was trained as a reconnaissance pilot. In May of that year he joined Escadrille C 47, flying Caudron G IIIs and G IVs. During his nearly two year stay with this unit, Fonck managed to achieve two confirmed 'kills', comprising a two-seat Rumpler and a single-seat Albatros D III. Shortly after this second victory Fonck was transferred to the then SPAD S VII-equipped Escadrille SPA 103, part of the famed Groupe de Chasse 12, 'Les Ciognes', or Storks. Fonck, always cool and calculating, went to work building his nationally unsurpassed tally of 75 confirmed victories, aided by an almost uncanny degree of marksmanship. The opposite of the impetuous Nungesser, Fonck, like many of his fellow French aces, preferred to stalk his victims alone, sending them to their fate with clinical precision. Fonck survived the war as France's leading air ace. Staying in aviation, Fonck twice failed to make the first west-to-east transatlantic crossing in 1926 and 1927, narrowly avoiding his own premature end in the crash of his big Sikorsky S-35 on 20 September 1926. Between 1937 and 1939, Fonck served as the French Air Force's Inspector of Fighter Aviation, prior to becoming a high profile emissary for the Vichy French regime. Fonck died, largely unsung, in June 1953. (Cowin Collection)

Below Developed directly from the SPAD VII, the prototype **SPAD XIII** flew initially on 4 April 1917. Because of the high degree of commonality with its forebear, the S XIII required the minimum of flight testing and therefore could go straight into production, ensuring that initial deliveries were flowing to operational units by the end of May 1917. With its more powerful 235hp Hispano-Suiza 8 Be, the S XIII could carry two synchronised .303 inch Vickers gun and still reach the much higher top level speed of 138mph at 6,560 feet. Standardised as the prime fighter type with both the French and American Expeditionary Forces, no less than 8,472 S XIIIs were to be built by the time of the Armistice. The machine seen here is carrying Le Prieur rocket projectiles attached to its inboard interplane struts for anti-balloon or anti-airship missions. (Cowin Collection)

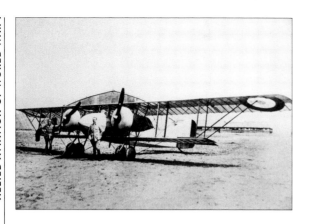

was doubled on entering service. One of the features that endeared the 2A.2 to its crews was its 'get homeability', its extremely robust structure capable of withstanding severe combat damage and still staying together. In all, around 3,200 examples of the 2A.2s were built, mainly for the French, but with deliveries of 705 to the Americans commencing in April 1918. (Cowin Collection)

Above Deployed as a successor day bomber to the Voisins in early 1917, the twin 120hp Le Rhone-powered **Caudron G VI** soon proved not up to penetrating deep into hostile airspace and was rapidly relegated to artillery observation, being replaced at the front by French-built Sopwith 1¹/₂ Strutters. Top level speed of the G VI was 94mph at 6,560 feet, while its maximum bomb load was 506lb. The G VI's defensive armament comprised one or two .303-inch flexibly mounted Lewis guns. (Cowin Collection)

Below and opposite, top Although more workmanlike than beautiful in their appearance, the **Breguet Bre 14** series of two seaters was deservedly destined to become the standard French long-range reconnaissance and day bomber during the closing year of the war. Almost directly comtemporary and certainly comparable to Britain's Airco DH 4/DH 9 series, the prototype Bre 14 first flew in November 1916 and following the completion of testing was ordered into quantity production for the French in March 1917. Initial operational deployment followed in September 1917. Powered mainly by the 300hp Renault, the shortage of these units sometimes led to the use of the 300hp Fiat A.12bis engine, the Bre 14A, seen here on the ground, was the reconnaissance version, with the Bre 14B being the bomber variant. While both versions had a top level speed of around 121mph at sea level, the operational

Below The **Salmson 2A.2** made its prototype debut in April 1917, entering operations towards the close of 1917. As it transpired this Salmson two-seater turned out to be one of France's finest reconnaissance types, quite capable of deep penetration beyond the front and fighting its way out when called upon to do so. Powered by a Salmson-built Canton-Unne radial, the 2A.2 had a top level speed of 115mph at 6,560 feet, along with an endurance of up to 3 hours. Armed initially with a single, fixed forward firing .303-inch Vickers in the nose and a flexibly mounted .303-inch Lewis in the rear, this armament

ceiling of the lighter loaded reconnaissance machine was 19,000 feet, while that of the bomber, with its up to 580lb bomb load and heavier defensive fire power of four, instead of three .303-inch guns, was reduced to 14,000 feet. The bomber, with its full load range of 280 miles, cruised at around 95mph. For short-range night missions, the Bre 14B could carry up to a 1,080lb bomb load. Belated as it was, the arrival of the Bre14B was to be welcomed by French bomber crews, as it finally ended the all-too lengthy period during which successive French bomber designs had almost invariably proven inadequate to their task. The Bre 14, successor to the French-built Sopwith 1½ Strutters, proved quite capable of being flown aggressively. Ernst Udet, Germany's second ranking fighter ace, nearly lost his life to one in March 1918. By the time of the Armistice, all French day bomber squadrons were operating Bre 14Bs, with no less than 55 French squadrons using the series. In addition to the French, the Bre 14 series was used by the Americans, who bought 290, along with the Belgians. Over 8,000 of the series were to be built in all, including considerable sub-contracted production by Darracq, Farman and Paul Schmitt. The impressive low-level fly-past image seen here is of a Bre 14B.2 belonging to Escadrille BR 111. Incidentally, the large transparent panel positioned under the observer's cockpit, on both sides of the fuselage, was the primary external means of identifying the bomber version from the 'recce' machines that lacked this feature. (Cowin Collection)

Below Despite the massive popularity of the Bre 14 with land-based crews, the type was only built in small numbers in its **Breguet Bre 14H** floatplane form for the French Navy, who primarily employed it in the reconnaissance role. The enormous width of the central pontoon is clearly visible in this view. (Cowin Collection)

The Factory's and Other People's Efforts

Britain, at the outbreak of war, did not have a recognizable aircraft industry, particularly when compared with that which existed in France. Indeed, as mentioned earlier, Britain would have been extremely hard pressed to mount any form of air combat activity without the very significant material support of the French industry, both in terms of airframes and engines, for the first two years of the conflict.

What Britain did have at the outset of war were two rival air arms, one the RFC, or Royal Flying Corps, controlled by the War Office, while the Admiralty controlled the RNAS, or Royal Naval Air Service.

Neither were adequately manned, equipped or funded by major European Power standards and to compound the problems Britain faced, the procurement and operating policies of the two air arms were frequently seen as being totally incompatible. In part, these differences flowed from the variance in the envisaged operational role of the RFC compared with the RNAS.

The War Office and senior Army staff saw the aeroplane almost exclusively as a useful, high-speed, range extending scouting adjunct, particularly useful to the artillery and cavalry. They had one particular 'bee-in-their-bonnet' and that was the constant demand for inherently stable flying machines. Discussed in greater depth in the preface to *X-Planes*, the first in this series

of books, suffice to say here that up to and including the first half of 1915, the War Office's attitude on this topic, mirrored to a large degree by the products coming out of the government-owned Royal Aircraft Factory, was that 'If God had intended aeroplanes to turn then he would have given them the means from the start.' Sadly, this steadfast adherence to stability at all cost was to be paid for by the loss of many BE 2 crew's lives as their slow and unmanoeuvrable mounts fell prey to the guns of the Fokker Eindekkers during the autumn of 1915. When their War Office masters eventually did wake up to the need for agility, the Royal Aircraft Factory, as in developing the RE 8, the BE 2's successor, initially made the machine just a little too unstable, particularly at low speed, resulting in a significant number of crashes caused by the aircraft 'spinning-in'.

More positively, the Royal Aircraft Factory's efforts would provide research into aircraft handling problems and the implementation of improvements in design and practice; and they kept British aircraft builders advised of any such advances. Indeed, it was this applied research and development effort, including continuous aircraft and aero-engine design that were to be the bedrock of the Royal Aircraft Factory effort once the war had started, with the mass of their aircraft and engine production being sub-contracted out.

How the Royal Aircraft Factory eventually sub-contracted much of its airframe work out points to the salient difference between the RFC's and RNAS's attitude towards British aircraft builders. Certainly for the first fifteen or so months of the war, the RFC and its Royal Aircraft Factory associate saw fit to place sub-contract work only, while the RNAS not only bought their aircraft from the aircraft manufacturer, they often asked them to develop the design in the first place.

Thus, while the Royal Aircraft Factory put out much of its work to such as Armstrong Whitworth, Boulton Paul, Blackburn, Bristol, Napier, Weir and Vickers – and these were just some of the BE 2 sub-contractors – little or no design work ever left the Factory.

When the War Office eventually relinquished its total control over the design and development aspect, this usually ended with the RFC buying an aircraft type originally drawn up to an Admiralty requirement, such as in the case of the Sopwith 1½ Strutter. Just how much more flexible the Admiralty's policies were to be forms the subject of a later chapter.

Left Officialdom's interference has often been cited as one of the main obstacles to aircraft development and certainly this was the case with Britain's **Airco DH 9**. This successor to the very successful day bomber DH 4, first deployed in March 1917, should have been a simple re-design of the fuselage centre section to place the pilot further back and far closer to the observer. Instead of this straightforward improvement, the War Office, in its wisdom, also chose to fit a totally new and untried engine to the DH 9. The ongoing troubles with this engine ensured that the later machine was generally inferior to its predecessor in virtually all operational aspects except crew communications. (British Official/Crown Copyright)

Above Lt Harvey-Kelley, seen puffing his cigarette as he studies the map beside his **Royal Aircraft Factory BE 2a**, serial no 347. Harvey-Kelley and his machine were the first of Britain's aviation expeditionary forces to land in France during the second week of the war. The BE 2a's 70hp Renault gave the two-seater reconnaissance type a top level speed of 70mph at sea level. The ceiling of the early BE 2s was around 10,000 feet, along with an endurance of about 3 hours. (British Official/Crown Copyright)

Above This **Royal Aircraft Factory BE 2c**, serial no 9951, is one of a known 111-aircraft batch built by Blackburn. This variant made its operational debut in April 1915 and was a marked improvement over the earlier BE 2s, using ailerons, rather than wing warping. Fitted with a 90hp Royal Aircraft Factory-developed RAF 1a engine, the two-seat BE 2c had a top level speed of 72mph at 6,500 feet, dropping to 69mph at 10,000 feet. Besides its primary reconnaissance role, the BE 2 served as a bomber, an anti-submarine patroller and a trainer. Deliveries of the BE 2c to the RFC accounted for 1,117 machines, plus a further 307 operated by the RNAS, of which the aircraft seen here was one. (Blackburn)

Opposite A future fighter ace in the making. This image of the nineteen-year-old Second Lieutenant **Albert Ball** shows him standing in front of a Caudron G III of the Ruffy-Baumann School of Flying at Hendon during the summer of 1915. As was the British Army practice of the day, any officer wishing to transfer to the RFC had to pay for his own initial flying training, only being reimbursed once he had gained his Aero Club Aviator's Certificate. Born in August 1896, Albert Ball was barely eighteen when commissioned into the Sherwood Forresters during October 1914. Determined to fly, Ball gained his Aviator's Certificate on 15 October 1915. Further flying training with the RFC brought Ball his military wings in January 1916. Ball joined his first operational unit, No 13 Squadron, RFC, at Vert Galand, France, flying the BE 2c, in February 1916. Three months later, in May 1916, Ball joined No 11 Squadron, RFC, a single-seater unit at Savy, flying Nieuport 16s and Bristol Scouts. Between then and October 1916, when Ball was sent home to instruct he had been promoted to Lieutenant and credited with a confirmed 31 'kills' In April 1917, Ball, now a Captain and 'A' Flight Commander of the newly formed, crack No 56 Squadron, RFC, flying SE 5s, returned to the Western Front. In the less than two week period between 23 April 1917 and 6 May 1917, Ball was to down a further 13 of the enemy, to bring his total confirmed score to 44. On the following evening of 7 May 1917, Ball's SE 5a was seen to break out of cloud base in an inverted spin and crash. Although Ball had been in combat with machines of Jasta 11, his death has been attributed to vertigo, or being knocked unconscious by a loose Lewis gun ammunition drum – the former being less likely than the latter which was a known hazard to Nieuport and SE 5 pilots. Ball, already the holder of a Military Cross, Distinguished Service Order and Bar, was posthumously awarded Britain's highest military award for gallantry, the Victoria Cross. (Cowin Collection)

Below The two seat **Vickers FB 5**, popularly known as the 'Gun Bus', had its origins in a visionary 1912 Admiralty requirement for a so-called fighting aeroplane, armed with a machine gun. The contract for this machine was placed with Vickers on 19 November 1912, where its development became somewhat protracted, the first production FB 5s, by now ordered for both the RFC and the RNAS, not reaching No 6 Squadron, RFC until November 1914, while the handful of RNAS FB 5s did not reach the front until early 1915. Powered by a somewhat unreliable 100hp Gnome Monosoupape, the FB 5's top level speed was 70mph at 5,000 feet, while the time taken to reach that altitude was 16 minutes. Excluding prototypes, around 136 FB 5s are known to have been produced by Vickers in Britain and Darracq in France. (Vickers)

Below During the last weeks of 1913, Frank Barnwell of Bristol's 'X' Department, drew up his first aircraft design. This machine, initially known as the Baby Biplane, became the Scout when demonstrated to the British Army in February 1914. With relatively minor modifications, this prototype was developed into the Scout B, of which the War Office bought two, followed by the Scout C, the first of the series to entered full scale produc-

tion in late 1914 for both the RFC and the RNAS. The 110hp Clerget or Le Rhone powered **Bristol Scout D**, seen here, made its debut in November 1915. Armed with an overwing mounted single .303-inch Lewis gun, the Scout D had a top level speed of 110mph at sea level and entered operational service in February 1916. The RFC and the RNAS each took delivery of 80 Scout Ds. (Bristol)

Above Clearly influenced by the success of the Sopwith Tabloid and Bristol Scout, the **Martinsyde S 1** prototype unarmed single-seat scout emerged during the late summer of 1914. Initially, the S 1 had a clumsy-looking four wheel landing gear, happily replaced by the time this machine, serial no 4241, was photographed. With an 80hp Gnome rotary, the S 1's top level speed was 87mph at sea level and its performance was generally considered inferior to both of its illustrious forebears. Only 61 S 1s were built, with deliveries to the RFC lasting for about a year between late 1914 and October 1915. Never to equip a complete squadron, S 1s were used by five French-based RFC squadrons, plus another RFC squadron in Mesopotamia. (Cowin Collection)

THE FACTORY'S AND OTHER PEOPLES' EFFORTS

Above The two seat **Royal Aircraft Factory RE 7**, first flown in early 1915, was employed in a variety of roles, ranging from its original task of light bomber, to reconnaissance, and escort fighter. Deliveries of the RE 7 started towards the close of 1915, the type making its operational debut with No 21 Squadron, RFC, on 23 January 1916. Not a great operational success due largely to the gunner being seated forward, where wings and struts restricted both his vision and field of fire, the type was withdrawn from front-line use by the end of 1916. Using a 150hp RAF 4a, the RE 7's top level speed was 82mph at 7,000 feet, while its maximum bomb load was 336lb. In all. 244 RE 7s were delivered to the RFC. (RAE Farnborough/ Crown Copyright)

Below The **Royal Aircraft Factory RE 8** was selected for mass production before the prototype's first flight in the spring of 1916. Powered by a 150hp RAF 4a, this two-seat reconnaissance bomber was not a very impressive performer with a top level speed of 103mph at 5,000 feet, falling off to 96.5mph at 10,000 feet. Its bomb load was 260lb. To compound the problems, the early RE 8s were prone to 'spin-in' if mishandled and even when this problem was remedied by adding ventral fin

area, the 'Harry Tate', as it was nicknamed, proved sadly lacking in agility, making it relatively easy prey for its German opponents. Its first operational deployment was with No 52 Squadron, RFC, in November 1916. The RE 8's armament consisted of a fixed .303-inch Vickers for the pilot, plus one or two flexibly mounted .303-inch Lewis guns for the observer. Some later machines used the 150 hp Hispano-Suiza, being referred to as the RE 8a. A total of 4,077 RE 8s were to be built, all but 22 Belgian-operated aircraft going to the RFC. This is a standard production RE 8. (British Official/Crown Copyright)

Below The two seat **Royal Aircraft Factory FE 2b** was designed as a fighter, reconnaissance and night bomber and was a 120hp, later 160hp Beardmore-engined development of the 1913 FE 2a. The first FE 2b flew initially during March 1915, the type entering operations two months later, with No 6 Squadron, RFC, based at Abeele. Initial delivery build-up was slow, with only 32 having been handed over by the end of 1915. Sadly, British pilots were to suffer badly at the hands of the Fokker Eindekkers thanks to this delay, as the FE 2B, along with the Airco DH 2, was to be pivotal in ending the Fokker scourge. Despite its poor top level speed of 91.5mph at sea level, the FE 2b's clear forward arcs of fire more than compensated. In all, 1,939 examples, including some converted FE 2a, were to be built. Serial no 5201, seen here, was the first of 50 Boulton Paul-built machines. (Dowty Boulton Paul)

Above Added protection for this **Royal Aircraft Factory FE 2d** came in the form of a second, pedestal-mounted .303-inch Lewis gun just ahead of the pilot. Operated by the front-seated observer, this flexibly trained weapon provided him with an upwards and rearwards arc of fire. Also noteworthy in this image is the long focal depth reconnaissance camera that the observer is pretending to sight. (British Official/Crown Copyright)

Opposite, left **James Thomas Byford McCudden** is seen here seated in the cockpit of his Royal Aircraft Factory SE 5a. McCudden, born on 25 March 1895 in Gillingham, Kent, came up through the enlisted ranks to became Britain's most highly decorated airman of World War I. Entering the British Army's Royal Engineers as a boy bugler in 1910, McCudden was to die a major six years later. As with a number of other fighter aces from both sides of the line, McCudden's flying career started as an observer and graduated into piloting two seat Royal Aircraft Factory FE 2d reconnaissance machines with No 20 Squadron, RFC in July 1916 for a few days, prior to joining the single seat Airco DH 2-equipped No 29 Squadron, RFC, on 1 August 1916. Before the month was through, McCudden, a cool, analytical pilot, had opened his tally of downed enemy aircraft by dispatching a two-seat Hannover Cl III. Indeed, McCudden, like Manfred von Richthofen and many other aces, tended to specialise in stalking two seaters, 'killing' no less than 45 of these machines out of his confirmed overall score of 57. Commissioned on 1 January 1917, McCudden was invited to join the hand-picked Royal Aircraft Factory SE 5a-equipped No 56 Squadron, RFC, joining the unit as a Captain and Flight

Commander on 15 August 1917. By the end of 1917, McCudden had taken his victory score to 37, adding a further 20 between 1 January 1918 and 16 February 1918, when he was posted home. On 6 April 1918, McCudden, already the proud holder of the Distinguished Service Order and bar, the Military Cross and bar, along with the Military Medal, was awarded Britain's highest military recognition for valour, the Victoria Cross. On 9 July 1918, the newly promoted Major James McCudden, Commanding Officer designate of No 60 Squadron, RFC, suffered an engine failure on take off for France, spinning in to his death while attempting to return to the airfield. (British Official/Crown Copyright)

Below and bottom The prototype **Airco DH 1** two seater, serial no 4220, seen here at Hendon and still without any form of markings was first flown in late January 1915. While this machine used a 70hp Renault, the subsequent 49 DH 1s, used as trainers, were fitted with an 80hp Renault. When later hard pressed to counter the Fokker Eindekker threat, the RFC asked Airco to look at converting their DH 1 into a reconnaissance fighter by using a 120hp Beardmore and adding a flexibly mounted .303-inch Lewis gun for the observer in the nose. Known as the **Airco DH 1a**, the uprated type was flight tested by Martlesham Heath against the Royal Aircraft Factory FE 2b, which it simply outflew. Regrettably, for the DH 1a, the FE 2b was already in large-scale production and, thus, only 50 machines were to be built, most of which went to training units. The gun-equipped DH 1a shown here carried the serial no 4607 and was the second of six to see service from June 1916 with No 14 Squadron, RFC, based in Palestine. (both de Havilland)

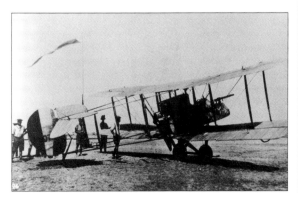

cross to the continent. Hawker's award of the Distinguished Service Order followed his daring raid on the airship sheds at Gontrode in Belgium during April 1915. At this time, the equipment of RFC squadrons included a mix of single- and two-seater aircraft and, along with others, Hawker experimented with arming the single-seat scouts, culminating in his mounting a .303-inch Lewis gun over the wing of a Bristol Scout C, serial no 1611. This technique allowed the gun to fire along the boresight axis of the aircraft, but above the top of the propeller arc, eliminating the need for gun interrupter or synchronising gear. It was while flying 1611, on 25 July 1916, that Hawker shot down three enemy aircraft all in the one day, to win the Victoria Cross. At the close of 1915, Hawker was given command of No 24 Squadron, RFC, then equipping with the new, single-seat Airco DH 2 pusher-engined fighter. Between March and November 1916, No 24 Squadron was in the forefront of the successful joint Anglo-French efforts to wrest back air superiority from the Germans, the unit, alone, accounting for 70 downed enemy machines. Meanwhile, Hawker, promoted to Major in February 1916, was forbidden to cross the lines by his superiors. However, On 23 November 1916, Hawker chose to ignore the restriction and, after a dogfight lasting nearly half an hour, died at the hands of Manfred von Richthofen, flying one of the new Albatros D IIs, against which his DH 2 was no match. Hawker is credited with 7 confirmed 'kills', all gained while he was with No 6 Squadron. (British Official/Crown Copyright)

Above Major **Lanoe George Hawker**, VC, DSO, was the first of Britain's fighter aces. Born on 30 December 1890, Hawker was commissioned into the Royal Engineers in 1911 and underwent pilot training in 1912. Completing the course in March 1913, Hawker was with No 6 Squadron, RFC, at the outbreak of war and was among the first wave of British military fliers to

Below and opposite, top First flown on 1 June 1915, 450 **Airco DH 2s** were to be built. Derived directly from the DH 1, the small, single seat DH 2 carried a single nose mounted .303-inch Lewis gun in its nose. On the prototype, the unorthodox mounting for the gun proved to be virtually useless and all subsequent DH 2s employed a gun, fixed in azimuth and only free to swing in elevation. Powered by a 100hp Gnome, or 110hp Le Rhone, the DH 2 had an unremarkable top level

Deliveries of these G 100s started early in 1916, with many going in twos and threes to serve as the escort sections of four RFC bomber squadrons in France and six in the Middle East. Indeed, only one unit, No 27 Squadron, RFC, was to be exclusively equipped with the type. With a top level speed of 97mph at sea level and lacking agility and pilot visibility, the G 100 was soon switched to bombing duties, thanks to its 5.5 hour endurance and ability to carry a 230lb bomb load. Around another 200 of the 160hp Beardmore powered single seat G 102 reconnaissance bombers were subsequently produced. (British Official/Crown Copyright)

speed of 93mph, but more than made up this shortfall by its agility that made it more than a match for the Fokker Eindekkers. Ironically, the Germans were to gain greater and earlier knowledge of the DH 2 than most RFC pilots would have for months yet, when the prototype fell into their hands at the end of July 1915, almost immediately after arriving in France for operational evaluation by No 5 Squadron, RFC. As it was, the first of the DH 2 deliveries were to No 24 Squadron, Lanoe Hawker's unit, at the end of 1915. While never completely free from potentially catastrophic engine-related problems, the DH 2 did well enough against the Fokkers, but was kept in front-line service long after the Germans had introduced the superior Albatros D II and D III. The large image is of the ill-starred prototype, while the small view shows one of the initial 100 aircraft batch production series. (both de Havilland)

Above First flown on 8 November 1915, the Royal Aircraft Factory **FE 8** was a pusher-engined, single seat fighter that was already obsolescent when the first deliveries were made to No 29 Squadron, RFC, in mid-June 1916. Powered by a 110hp Le Rhone or Clerget rotary, giving the machine a top level speed of 97mph at sea level, its armament comprised a single .303-inch Lewis gun. 297 FE 8s are known to have been built. The FE 8, serial no 7624, seen here being inspected by its German captors, was photographed near Provin on 9 November 1916. (Cowin Collection)

Below First flown in September 1915, the prototype **Martinsyde G 100,** serial no 4735, was a single-seat, long range fighter using a 120hp Beardmore with fuselage flanking radiators. This machine was followed by 100 production G 100s, whose engines had a much cleaner nose-mounted radiator. The G 100's effective armament was a single, overwing .303-inch Lewis gun, although a second, rearward-firing Lewis gun was fitted, presumably more in hope than expectation.

Above and below The then Captain **William Avery Bishop**, photographed both in the cockpit of his No 60 Squadron, RFC, Nieuport 17, serial no B 1556 and standing beside it. Destined to survive World War I with a confirmed score of 72 victories, 'Billy' Bishop was born in Ontario, Canada, on 8 February 1894, Bishop was already a Lieutenant with a Canadian cavalry unit at the outbreak of war. As with other aces-to-be, Bishop started his flying career as an observer in Royal Aircraft Factory RE 7s of No 21 Squadron, RFC, during the autumn of 1915. Hospitalised with a knee injury sustained in a crash landing early in 1916, Bishop then underwent pilot training, following which he spent the rest of the year and early 1917 flying the Royal Aircraft Factory BE 2c with a UK-based anti-airship unit. In mid-March 1917, the young Canadian was posted to No 60 Squadron, RFC, operating Nieuports over the Western Front. Just over a week later, 'Billy' Bishop was to score his first 'kill'.

During the next five months, Bishop's tally rose to 36, with his lone 2 June 1917 attack on a German airfield earning him the coveted Victoria Cross for exceptional bravery. After an enforced extended leave back in Canada, Major Bishop, as he now was, returned to France in mid-March to command the Royal Aircraft Factory SE 5a-equipped No 85 Squadron, RFC. Between then and 19 June 1918, 'Billy' Bishop doubled his score of confirmed victories before being effectively forced to quit operational flying for public relations reasons. Bishop returned to Canada after the war, where he helped create the Royal Canadian Air Force, becoming an Air Vice Marshal in the process. 'Billy' Bishop died on 11 September 1956 (both British Official/Crown Copyright)

Opposite, top Despite the Admiralty's early initiative to employ their Avro 504s in the bombing role, albeit only carrying four 20lb Hale bombs apiece, the general adoption of the Royal Aircraft Factory BE 2c reconnaissance bomber by both the British services nearly ended the Avro 504 story in its infancy. Happily, someone in high places decided to give the old warhorse a further lease of life as the standard British military trainer. Fitted with a 110hp Le Rhone, the **Avro 504K** could reach a top level speed of 95mph at sea level and climb to 8,000 feet in 6.5 minutes. Including early 504 production, many of which were converted to 504Ks, around 5,440 examples were built under World War I contracts. After a pause in the immediate post-war years, more were to follow. Avro 504K, serial no E3404, seen here, was the first of a batch of 500 built by the parent company. Many more of the 504Ks built were produced by numerous sub-contractors. (Avro)

Below Essentially an Admiralty sponsored design, carrying their Type 9700 designation, the **Sopwith 1¹/₂Strutter** has already been touched upon in Chapter 2 and will be dealt with again in Chapter 4. Suffice to say here that the type was also operated by by the RFC. Serial no A 6901, seen here, was the first of a 100 aircraft batch produced by Hooper & Co Ltd of Chelsea for the RFC and is particularly interesting in being one of the only four single-seat home defence fighter variants built. (Hawker)

Below A direct, slightly smaller derivative of the Vickers FB 5, the two-seat **Vickers FB 9** proved to be another case of providing too little, too late, resulting in the type being largely relegated to the training role. First flown towards the end of 1915, the FB 9 used the same 100hp Gnome Monosoupape as its predecessor, providing the machine with an uncomfortably slow top level speed of 82.6mph at sea level, decreasing to 79mph at 6,500 feet. Even worse was the 19 minutes the aircraft took to reach this altitude. The FB 9's armament consisted of a single .303-inch Vickers gun mounted in the forward, or observer's cockpit. Of the 119 FB9s believed to have been built, including 24 for the RFC from Darracq in France, only two are known to have entered into operational service, both joining 'B' Flight of No 11 Squadron, RFC in June 1916. (Vickers)

Below The three seat **Airco DH 3** was to be the victim of an Air Board policy shift away from twin- to single-engined bombers. As a result, only one of the two prototypes ordered, serial no 7744, was completed and flown. Initially using two 120hp Beardmores, the machine proved somewhat underpowered and was re-engined to take the 160hp Beardmore as the DH 3a, the form in which it is seen here. First flown in April 1916, a contract for 50 production aircraft was cancelled in favour of the single-engined DH 4. Performance of the DH 3a included a top level speed of 95mph, a full military load of 680lb that included ammunition for the two .303-inch Lewis guns, along with a full load range of 700 miles. As it was, the experience gained with this machine was not totally wasted, the project being resurrected later in the form of the DH 10. (de Havilland)

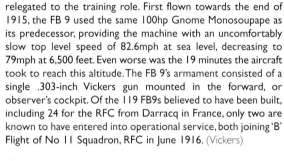

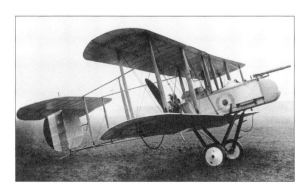

Above The sole **Vickers FB 14**, serial no A3505, served as the prototype for a desultory series of two-seat, general-purpose machines, ending in the FB 14F. Designed as successors to the Royal Aircraft Factory BE 2 series in Middle East service, these 1916 FB 14s employed a variety of engines, ranging from the 160hp Beardmore to the 250hp Rolls-Royce Eagle. An FB 14's top level speed was a reasonable 99.5mph at sea level, but its climb performance was truly frightening, taking nearly 41 minutes to reach 10,000 feet, which itself was only 600 feet below the machine's ceiling. Typical armament comprised the standard pilot's fixed Vickers gun, plus a flexible-mounted Lewis gun for the observer. While the performance of subsequent variants could only improve, even that of the 250hp-powered FB 14D appears unremarkable. Figures on just how many of the series were built vary from between 41 to 100, with reports that some actually reached Middle East-based RFC units. About the only real figure available involved seven FB 14Ds delivered to home defence squadrons. (Vickers)

Below The **Armstrong Whitworth FK 8** was a contemporary of the Royal Aircraft Factory's RE 8, being generally considered as the better of the pair. First flown in May 1916, the two-seat FK 8 reconnaissance bomber was initially powered by a 120hp Beardmore, soon replaced by its larger 160hp brother. Top level speed of the FK 8 was 98.4mph at sea level, decreasing to 88mph at 10,000 feet. Besides the standard .303-inch Vickers and Lewis gun combination, the FK 8 could

haul a bomb load of up to 160lb. The type made its operational debut with No 35 Squadron, RFC, on 24 January 1917, with deliveries flowing to another four French-based RFC squadrons, two in the Balkans, one in Palestine and to home defence units. Two pilots were to win the Victoria Cross flying the FK 8, while an FK 8 of Kent-based No 50 Squadron, RFC, is credited with downing a Gotha off the North Foreland on 7 July 1917. Some 1,000 or so FK 8s had been built when production ended in July 1918. (British Official/Crown Copyright)

Below The two seat **Bristol S 2A** fighter, a derivative of the Bristol Scout D was unusual in that it had the pilot and gunner placed side-by-side. Built originally to an Admiralty requirement, the first of the two built, serial no 7836 seen here, first flew in May 1916. Using a 110 Clerget, or 100 Gnome Monosoupape, the S 2A had a top level speed of 95mph at sea level. While not pursued as a fighter, both S 2As went on to serve as advanced trainers with the Central Flying School. (Bristol)

Opposite, top The term 'inertia' is normally applied to a physical object's resistance to any change of state in its motion, sometimes, however, the term is equally applicable to the mind-set of a company's management, as in the case of **Vickers' FB 12**. First flown in June 1916, the initial FB 12 used an 80hp Le Rhone, but production examples of this single-seat fighter were to have been powered by the 150hp Hart rotary. Following the failure of this engine, the FB 12, with its long-obsolete pusher-engined layout was fitted with a 110hp Le Rhone to become

the FB 12C. By the time the FB12C had flown it was the spring of 1917, subsequent flight trials showing the machine to have a top level speed of 87mph at a time when average fighter speeds exceeded 110mph. To add further to Vickers' troubles, the second FB 12C, serial no A 7352, seen here fitted with a 100hp Anzani was criticised by Martlesham Heath, in June 1917, as lacking sufficient pitch control at low speed and having generally heavy handling traits. Of the 50 production batch ordered, all but 18 were to be cancelled. (Vickers)

Right and below The development of the much-loved two-seat **Bristol F 2B** fighter, or 'Brisfit' for short, commenced during March 1916 around a 120hp Beardmore. Clearly, with this engine, the design was in serious danger of being underpowered and in July 1916, Bristol's Frank Barnwell was delighted to be offered the use of both the 150hp Hispano-Suiza and the 190hp Rolls-Royce Falcon to be fitted in his two **Bristol F 2A** prototypes for comparative testing. The first of these, serial no A 3303, seen here in its unfamiliar initial form, was fitted with the Rolls-Royce engine and first flew on 9 September 1916. By now, because of the unavailability of the Hispano-Suiza unit, it had already been decided to order 50 Falcon-powered production F 2As, delivery of which commenced on 20 December 1916. Even before this contract was completed a further 200 of the improved F 2B version were ordered, deliveries of which started on 13 April 1917. In the interim, No 48 Squadron, RFC, had been formed with F 2As, the unit going into action against the Albatros D IIIs of Manfred von Ricthofen's Jasta 11 on 5

April 1917. Using their F 2As quite inappropriately as gun platforms for their observers, No 48 Squadron took a mauling with the loss of four F 2As. Indeed, more losses were to follow during most of April until No 48's pilots realised the best way to fight with a 'Brisfit' was to use it as a single seater. From this point, the fortunes of the 'Brisfit' became legendary. No 11 Squadron, the first unit to form with F 2Bs, had one crew that downed 30 enemy aircraft between June 1917 and January 1918. By July 1917, it had been decided to standardise around the F 2B for all RFC fighter reconnaissance and corps reconnaissance squadrons. When equipped with the 275hp Rolls-Royce Falcon III, the top level speed of the F 2B was 125mph at sea level, the machine having a ceiling of 20,000 feet. The F 2B's armament comprised a single fixed Vickers gun for the pilot, along with one or two flexibly mounted Lewis guns for the observer. Besides this, the F 2B could carry an up to 240lb bomb load. Of the 5,250 F 2Bs ordered at the time of the Armistice, some 3,101 had been completed by the end of 1918. The F 2B also engendered interest in America, with a 300hp Hispano-Suiza powered version being proposed, but due to the inappropriate installation of a 400hp Liberty at the Curtiss plant, followed by the machine crashing, US interest waned until McCook Field demonstrated where the trouble lay, leading to the post-war production of 40 Hispano-Suiza-powered Dayton Wright-built F 2Bs. The image of the F 2B chosen here is of serial no A 7231, captured by Fl Abt 210 near Cambrai, during the summer of 1917. (Bristol and Cowin Collection)

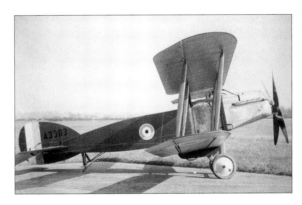

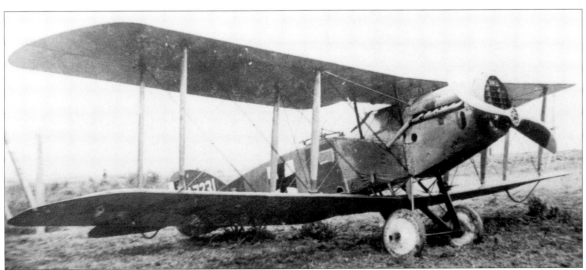

Above Developed from the company's sole M 1A and the four M 1Bs, the first of which made its maiden flight on 14 July 1916, the **Bristol M 1C** was the only British front-line combat type to use a monoplane configuration during World War 1 and clearly represented an opportunity lost. Considered by official-dom as having too high a landing speed, at 49mph, for use on the Western Front, the M 1C's deployment was confined to partially equipping five Middle East-based RFC squadrons, thus only 125 M 1Cs were built between September 1917 and February 1918. Armed with a single .303-inch Vickers gun, the M 1C, powered by a 110hp Le Rhone, was capable of a top level speed of 130mph at sea level and of operating at up to 20,000 feet. Reputed to have good overall handling characteristics, this appears to be borne out from the fact that M 1Cs were highly sought after as senior flight officers' hacks. (Cowin Collection)

Below and above right The two seater **Airco DH 4**, first flown in mid-August 1916, was to prove one of the finest fast light bombers of World War 1. Using a variety of engines, whose outputs ranged from 190hp to 375hp, the typical late production DH 4, of which A 7995 seen here is an example, used a 250hp Rolls-Royce Eagle III, giving it a top level speed of 119mph at 6,500 feet, along with a ceiling of 16,000 feet. The first unit to deploy the DH 4 operationally was No 55 Squadron, RFC, on 6 March 1917. Typically, the DH 4's warload

was four 112 lb bombs, but two 230lb weapons could be carried. Used by both the RFC and the RNAS, armaments varied, with RFC machines carrying the standard two-seater fit of a single Vickers and a single Lewis gun, while in the RNAS DH 4s the armament was doubled at some cost in perfor-mance. One major shortfall with the DH 4 was the lack of communications between pilot and observer, solved in the near identical DH 9 airframe by bringing them closer. In all, Airco and five sub-contractors were to build 1,538 DH 4s, a figure dwarfed by US production dealt with separately in Chapter 6. The smaller image above is of A 7845, a reconnaissance fighter version of the DH 4 used by No 202 Squadron, RAF. Note the ventral fairing required to house the long focal length camera. (both de Havilland)

Opposite Resplendent in his RFC Captain's uniform **Geoffrey de Havilland** is seen here beside the Airco DH 9 that he had designed. Born the son of a clergyman in 1882, Sir Geoffrey, as he was to become, entered the automotive industry for a few short years before contracting the 'aviation bug' in 1908. Armed with £1,000 advanced by his father and with the help of his friend, Frank Herle, de Havilland built a canard biplane with a 45hp Iris engine built to his design. With this machine, de Havilland managed to make one short hop before it was 'writ-ten-off' in December 1908. In 1910, de Havilland produced his second design, which while offering little novelty, had the great

attribute of actually flying, its first flight taking place on 10 September 1910. It was with this machine that the young designer/pilot taught himself to fly. Already married, Geoffrey de Havilland was no doubt pleased when his work came to the attention of the War Office, who bought his second biplane for £400 and took him on as an aeroplane designer and test pilot at Farnborough's Royal Balloon Factory. Here, working in harness with the Factory's design engineer, Frederick Green, De Havilland transformed a number of dubious flying machines into useful aircraft, starting with the FE 2 and culminating in the spectacularly advanced BS 1, later rebuilt as the SE 2A and discussed in Chapter 1. Growing unhappy at the now renamed

Royal Aircraft Factory, de Havilland resigned in June 1914 to join Thomas Holt's Airco as their Chief Designer, where, with the exception of a short break to join the RFC later that year, he was to stay until 1920 and the dissolution of the company. During this time, he not only designed the DH 1 through DH 18, he also took them up for their first flights. On 25 September 1920, he and colleagues were to found the de Havilland Aircraft Company. Producers of many famous aircraft, including the ubiquitous Mosquito of World War II and the post-war Comet jetliner, this company was to emblazon the skies with the de Havilland name. Sir Geoffrey, who had lost two of his three sons in flying accidents, died in 1965. (de Havilland)

Below The de Havilland designed single-seater **Airco DH 5**, characterised by its novel back-staggered wing arrangement chosen to improve pilot visibility, was to prove a disappointment. Completed during the autumn of 1916, the DH 5 was found to lack performance above 10,000 feet, as well as being tricky to land. These problems, coupled to severe delivery delays with the DH 5's 110hp Le Rhone 9J, saw the type's role being relegated from fighter to ground attack and production being limited to 550 aircraft. Initially delivered to No 24 Squadron, RFC, in May 1917, the DH 5's top level speed was 102mph at 10,000 feet, decreasing to 89mph at 15,000 feet. Armament was a single .303-inch Vickers – somewhat puny for trench strafing – while the machine's overall performance compared poorly to that of the Sopwith Pup already in service. The DH 5 seen here belonged to No 68 Squadron, RFC, based at Baizieux. (British Official/Crown Copyright)

Below The **Royal Aircraft Factory SE 5**, powered by a 150hp direct drive Hispano-Suiza, initially took to the skies on 22 November 1916. Carrying a two-gun armament of one fixed, nose mounted, synchronised .303-inch Vickers, plus a .303-inch Lewis mounted above the wing that could be locked to fire ahead of the aircraft, or freed to swing through a limited arc of elevation, enabling the pilot to rake an enemy's underside. Virtually viceless in terms of pilot handling problems and capable of 122mph at 3,000 feet, decreasing to 116mph at 10,000 feet. The operational ceiling of the SE 5 was 17,000 feet, while the single seater could reach 10,000 feet in 13 minutes 40 seconds. Most of the 59 SE 5s built went to No 56 Squadron, RFC, commencing in March 1917, prior to their appearance on the Western Front the following month. These interim SE 5s were soon to be replaced by the more powerful SE 5a, arguably the finest of Britain's World War I fighters. This rearward aspect

Right Ultimately to be credited with 73 'kills' made over the relatively short span of fourteen and a half months, **Edward Mannock**, born in 1887, had been interned by the Turks at the outbreak of war and only his failing health led to his repatriation. However, once home, the mild mannered Mannock lost little time in joining the British Army's Medical Corps from where he transferred to the RFC in August 1916: this despite his having a defective left eye! Mannock went on to gain his 'wings', at Hendon, on 28 November 1916. Mannock's first exposure to operational flying came on 1 April 1917, when he joined No 40 Squadron, RFC, flying Nieuport 17s from Treizennes, near St Omer. Just over a month later, on 7 May 1917 and now with No 74 Squadron, RFC, Mannock opened his victory score by downing an enemy observation balloon, no mean feat in itself, recalling that these artillery-directing aerostats were invariably heavily defended. Over the next ten months Mannock's tenacity brought him both recognition and promotion. On 18 June 1918, Edward Mannock, by now a major, took command of No 85 Squadron, RAF, freshly returned to the St Omer Front and equipped with Royal Aircraft Factory SE 5As. Mannock, on one single sortie in May 1918, took on a flight of six Pfalz single seaters, downing four of them. Destined not to survive the war, on 26 July 1918, a German infantryman's bullet was to pierce Mannock's fuel tank, turning his machine into a flaming torch that arced its way down behind German lines. At the time of his death, Mannock's confirmed score stood at 50 'kills', thanks to his generosity in attributing some of his score to others. This 'shortfall' in Mannock's record was subsequently rectified, the valiant aviator being posthumously awarded Britain's highest military honour, the Victoria Cross. (British Official/ Crown Copyright)

on SE 5, A8913 helps emphasise the use of broad chord ailerons on both upper and lower wings – a feature that improved the aircraft's 'rollability' (British Official/Crown Copyright)

Bottom Despite being beset with a series of engine-related problems the 200hp Hispano-Suiza-powered **Royal Aircraft Factory SE 5a** gave more than a good account of itself when measured against the later Fokker D VII and Pfalz D XII single seaters that it would encounter from the spring of 1918 onwards. With a top level speed of 137.5mph at sea level, plus an ability to reach 10,000 feet in 11 minutes, the first SE 5a operational deliveries commenced in June 1917. Sadly, the engine troubles, coupled to engine non-availability acted as a bottleneck to the numbers of SE 5as that could be fielded well into 1918, the problem only really being resolved with the emergence of the 200hp Wolseley Viper, a British development of the original French engine. Total SE 5 and SE 5a production reached 5,205 machines by war's end, with Curtiss in the US contracted to produce a further 1,000 for the Americans. While all but one of the Curtiss order were to be cancelled with the Armistice, 56 British SE 5a deliveries were made to the Americans. The SE 5a seen here is serial no B4897. (RAE/Crown Copyright)

Right Born on 27 September 1897, **Arthur Rhys-Davids'** career prospects looked promising, when, in late 1916, he was to join the RFC. With a scholarship place already secured for Oxford, this former head boy at Eton completed his pilot training in time to join the crack, Royal Aircraft Factory SE 5 equipped No 56 Squadron, RFC, preparing for its April 1917 departure to St Omer. At the front, Rhys-Davids, although a novice fighter pilot, demonstrated his ability to survive encounters with far more experienced foes before going on to notch

up a confirmed 25 victories, including the downing of Werner Voss, all within the span of a brief four months. Significantly. Of these 'kills' all but five were made during fighter-on-fighter combat. Hardly more than a boy, Lieutenant A.P.F. Rhys-Davids was to meet his own end on 27 October 1917, falling to the guns of Lt Karl Gallwitz of the famed Jasta Boelcke. (British Official/Crown Copyright)

Above and below First flown in March 1917, the **Sopwith 1F** Camel, like that of its precursor, the Pup, was the joint brain-child of Sopwith's pilot Harry Hawker and engineer Fred Sigrist. Unlike the Pup, however, the Camel never basked in its pilot's unmitigated delight at its handling, indeed, the Camel's capricious in-flight behaviour left not just much to be desired, but many young, inexperienced Camel pilots dead. The Camel's problems, which could also be used to effect by experienced fliers, stemmed from the fact that much of its mass, comprising engine, twin .303-inch Vickers guns, pilot and fuel, all lay within the first 7 feet of its overall 18.75 feet fuselage length, This, combined with the high torque reaction involved with its 130hp Clerget 9B rotary and, in particular, the short rudder moment arm, ensured that the machine turned to starboard, or the right, with breathtaking rapidity, while causing the nose to

drop. If this tight turn was not rapidly corrected with rudder, the aircraft would readily enter a spin from which it was diffi-cult to escape at low altitude. In the case of a turn to port, or to the left, the rate of turn was far less ferocious, while this time the nose rose. So long as he survived the initial familiari-sation phase of Camel flying, the pilot could then use these characteristics to effect, by using its 'instant' starboard turning capability to out-turn his enemy and, thus, rapidly position himself behind his foe. Operational deployment of the Camel came in July 1917, with deliveries of the machine going to both RFC and RNAS squadrons. The 1F Camel's top level speed of 115mph at 6,500 feet fell off to 106.5mph at 15,000 feet, while the single seater reached 10,000 feet in 10 minutes, 35 seconds while on its way to its 17,300 feet ceiling. Besides the standard Clerget, other rotaries were fitted to various 1F batches, rang-ing from 110hp Le Rhones to the 150hp Bentley BR 1. The smaller of the two images, left, is the Sopwith 1F Camel of No 139 Squadron, RFC's leader, the then Capt W.G. Barker, whose mount carried seven, rather than the unit's normal four fuse-lage white stripes aft of the roundel. To emphasise the Camel's unforgiving nature, the larger, rare image depicts Ser no B 3801, one of the three known Camels converted to two-seat train-ers during 1918, in an attempt to reduce the mounting number of fatalities encountered during type conversion flying. (both British Official/Crown Copyright)

Opposite, top Designed from the outset as a primary trainer, the **Airco DH 6** emerged early in 1917. Designed to be both easy to fly and repair, the early DH 6s were powered by a 90hp RAF 1A, but shortages of this engine led to the adoption of either the 80hp Renault or 90hp Curtiss OX-5. Top level speed of the DH 6 fitted with an RAF 1A, as seen here fitted to Serial no B2612, was 70mph, while the initial climb was a meagre 225 feet per minute. By late 1917, the DH 6 had been dropped in favour of the Avro 504K as the RFC's standard trainer, enabling more than 300 of the total 2,303 DH 6 and DH 6a production to be switched to the RNAS for anti-submarine coastal patrol work, carrying a 100lb bombload. (de Havilland)

Below The sole **Sopwith Bee** of 1917 was a diminutive single-seater, largely attributed to Harry Hawker. Powered by a 50hp Gnome, the small overall 16 feet 3 inch wingspan, coupled to its 14 feet 3 inch length could indicate that it was Sopwith's submission for a compact, shipboard fighter, but this cannot be confirmed. (Cowin Collection)

Right Readily distinguishable from the original FB 19, of August 1916, by its forward staggered upper wing, the **Vickers FB 19 Mk II** entered service in small numbers staring in June 1917. FB 19 Mk IIs served with No 17 Squadron, RFC, in Macedonia, while examples of this 100hp or 110hp rotary engined, single Vickers-gunned, single seater were known to have been flown by No.s 14 and 111 Squadrons in Palestine. As only 12 Mk IIs are known to have been built, it is clear that only sections of each squadron operated the type. Top level speed of the Mk II was 102mph at 10,000 feet, but its all-round performance was held to be unimpressive. (Vickers)

Below The anachronistic **Royal Aircraft Factory FE 9** two-seat reconnaissance fighter was powered by a pusher-mounted 200hp Hispano-Suiza and first flew in the early spring of 1917. As the Bristol F2B was already more than adequately meeting this requirement, it was not surprising that this design with its top level speed of 105mph at sea level, plus faltering climb that took 8 minutes 25 seconds to reach 5,000 feet was abandoned. The only machines to fly were the three development aircraft, the first of which, Serial no A 4818, is seen here. (RAE/Crown Copyright)

Above and below First flown at the end of May 1917, the **Sopwith 5F Dolphin** started life as a high altitude single-seat fighter design, but saw service as a close air support machine, with trench and ground strafing as its primary role. Built around its 200hp geared Hispano-Suiza, that was to prove so troublesome, the Dolphin incorporated a set of backward, or negatively staggered wings. Highly thought of by officialdom, the machine was ordered into quantity production shortly after its operational evaluation in mid-June 1917. By 31 December 1917, 121 Dolphins had been delivered to the RFC, whose No 19 Squadron was the first unit to re-equip with the type in January 1918. In operational service, the type was not best loved by its pilots, their criticisms centring on the lack of head and neck protection in the event of the machine 'nosing-over', coupled to the flexible 'crossbar' mounting of two upward-firing Lewis guns. This rather cumbersome device had the major drawback of allowing the guns to swing and strike the pilot in the face, not the ideal situation in any circumstances and particularly not when flying at low level. As these guns

supplemented twin, synchronised fixed Vickers guns, they were removed from most operational aircraft, with the exception of No 87 Squadron, who repositioned theirs atop the lower wings and outside the propeller arc. Top level speed of the Dolphin was 131mph at sea level. In October 1918, five Dolphins had been ordered for evaluation by the American Expeditionary Forces, but the cessation of hostilities soon afterwards ended this interest. At the time of the Armistice, while the engine-related problems had been overcome, only 600 or so of the 1,500 Dolphins airframes built by then had actually been delivered, the large part of the remainder awaiting the supply of engines. The larger image seen here is of the fourth prototype Dolphin and the first to incorporate the Dolphin's definitive shape. The close-up view of the same aircraft below left shows the 'crossbar' mounted, upward-firing Lewis guns that could prove so dangerous. (both Hawker)

Opposite, top In what appears to have been a classic example of snatching defeat from the jaws of victory the prototype **Airco DH 9** had been converted from a production DH4. This aircraft, first flown in August 1917, embodied a revised nose to take the new and still largely untested Siddeley Puma, along with the pilot's cockpit moved aft, far closer to the observer so as to improve crew communications, albeit at the expense of the pilot's forward visibilty. Even with these changes, quite a lot of commonality existed between the DH 9 and its precursor, which should have led to a minimum of production problems in switching between the two machines. This was not to be the case, with deliveries of the DH 9 only getting underway in January 1918, thanks in large part to the Puma engine that required de-rating from an originally envisaged 300hp to 230hp. To make matters worse, the loss of engine power affected performance to a serious degree, ensuring that the DH 9's capability was actually inferior to that of the DH 4. Despite this state of affairs, no less than 3,890 DH 9s were produced out of the 5,584 originally ordered, before production switched to the re-engined DH 9a. To some degree, the decision to press ahead

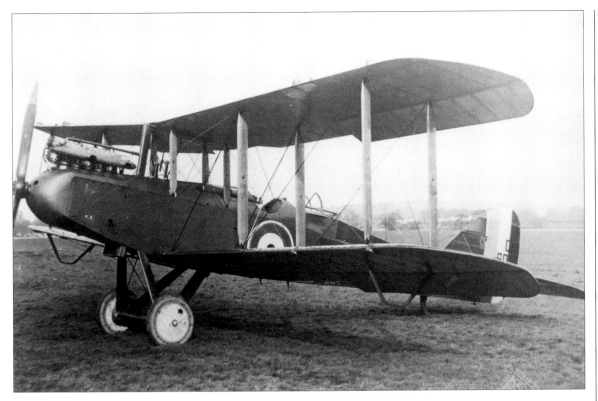

with production of such a disappointing machine could be explained by the pressure to expand the number of British bomber squadrons. The DH 9's full bomb load was 460lb and its top level speed was 109.5mph at 10,000 feet. The machine's ceiling was 15,500 feet, while its armament was the single Vickers gun for the pilot, plus the one or two flexibly-mounted Lewis guns for the observer. (de Havilland)

Below In the light of the DH 9's palpable failure, steps were initiated to replace the underpowered Siddeley Puma with something a little more powerful and tractable in the shape of the 375hp Rolls-Royce Eagle VIII, the work being given to Westland towards the end of 1917. Once flight testing got underway on the first **Airco DH 9a**, previously DH 9, serial no B 7664, seen here, good things transpired, with the injection of extra power boosting the two seater's top level speed to 125.5mph, from the DH 9's 114mph without bomb load and from 109.5mph to 118mph with full bomb load – all at 10,000

feet. First flight of the prototype DH 9a occured in February 1918, with initial deliveries of this reconnaissance bomber, to No 110 Squadron, RAF, following in August 1918. Sadly, at the time of the Armistice, only 885 examples of the DH 9a had been produced out of the 3,000 machines on order from Airco and five sub-contractors. Equally sadly for many DH 9 crews who were not to survive, the comparative handful of the much improved DH 9a machines that did reach the front arrived far too late. (de Havilland)

Below The diminutive **Sopwith Sparrow** of late 1917 used a 35hp ABC Gnat and was built for work into radio-controlled aircraft being done by Capt A.M. Low, RFC. Although a number of parallel studies were being carried out at this time into the use of radio-controlled, explosive-filled aircraft as guided missiles, the minimally sized and powered Sparrow was more probably aimed at providing one of the world's first evasive aerial targets. (Hawker)

Above The original **Sopwith 7F Snipe** single seat fighter bore a close resemblance to its precursor, the Camel, being first flown in this form during the autumn of 1917. It was not until January 1918 that the fourth of the six Snipe prototypes, serial no B 9965 seen here, was to emerge with what was to be the machine's definitive shape, with its 30 feet span double bay wings replacing the early example's single bay, 25 feet 9 inch span wing. B 9965 also employed the 230hp Bentley BR 2 rotary engine that was to become standard to the type. Interestingly, Martlesham Heath, who had responsibility for all service testing of military landplanes were guarded in their findings on the Snipe prototypes and it really took the enthusiasm of a St Omer-based lieutenant-colonel, who conducted the operational evaluation of B 9965 in mid-March 1918, to persuade his superiors to order the Snipe in large quantities. By the time initial production Snipes began to appear during the summer of 1918, the type had lost its overwing Lewis gun – its twin Vickers guns being considered sufficent – the tailplane had become adjustable in flight to relieve trim loads and both fin and rudder area were increased. Top level speed of the Snipe was 121mph at 10,000 feet, while it took 9 minutes 25 seconds to reach that altitude. The Snipe's ceiling was 19,500 feet. The first operational deployment of the Snipe was by No 43 Squadron, RAF, on 23 September 1918 and only a comparative handful of the 1,700 ordered had been delivered at the time of the Armistice. The lack of combat experience notwithstanding, the Snipe was to remain the RAF's standard single seat fighter through the mid-1920s. (Hawker)

Right **William Barker**, born in Manitoba, Canada, on 3 November 1894, joined up at the outbreak of war and sailed for Britain with the Canadian Mounted Rifles in the spring of 1915. By now a machine gunner, Barker went to the front in September 1915, transferring to the RFC, as a probationary observer in December 1915, where he joined No 9 Squadron, RFC and it was with this unit, that, in March 1916, Barker, from the back seat of his Royal Aircraft Factory BE 2c dispatched his first foe, a Fokker, to a fiery grave. Commissioned on 2 April 1916, Barker continued flying as an observer with Nos 4 and 15 Squadrons, RFC, prior to commencing pilot training towards the end of 1916. Gaining his 'wings' in January 1917, Barker

returned to France, where he flew two-seat Royal Aircraft Factory BE 2s and RE 8s until September 1917, when he was sent back to Britain to instruct. Unhappy with his lot, Barker, in October 1917, succeeded in transferring to Sopwith Camel-equipped No 28 Squadron, RFC, as 'A' Flight Commander. The unit itself was about to depart to help arrest Austrian gains on the Italian front. In Italy, Barker joined No 66 Squadron, RAF, early in the spring of 1918, prior to his return to the Western Front, in July 1918, to take command of No 139 Squadron, RAF, both of these units flying Camels. At this time Barker's confirmed 'kills' totalled 38 and at the end of September 1918, the illustrious Canadian was ordered back to Britain for a spell of instructing. Barker, as usual, fought with the powers-that-be, wresting from them the concession that, from time to time, he be allowed to return to the front 'to keep his eye in'. It was during his return flight from one of these visits to the front, that, on 27 October 1918, Major W. G. Barker was to win his

Victoria Cross. On this occasion, while flying Sopwith Snipe, serial no E 8102 and having departed La Targette, just east of Cambrai, Barker spotted and climbed to intercept a high flying Rumpler C VII two seater. Having dispatched the C VII with ease, Barker followed it down only to be surprised and wounded in the thigh by bullets from a Fokker Dr I, which he then shot down. Unfortunately, at this point, Barker found himself flying against around 16 Fokker D VIIs. With no alternative but to fight, Barker fought a solitary action in which he was further wounded, but miraculously managed to get both his bullet-riddled machine and himself back to the Allies' side of the lines. As a result of this action, Barker was credited with 4 'kills', plus 2 probables. Having survived the war with a confirmed score of 50 victories, Barker was to die in a flying accident on 12 March 1930. (British Official/Crown Cpyright)

ern seaboard in 1897, Rogers joined the RFC in 1916 and survived the war as a Captain, with a confirmed victory tally of 9, including the downing of the Gotha flown by Rudolf Klein, commanding officer of KG 3, on 12 December 1917 (see page 85 of the companion volume on German and Austrian Aviation). Happily, Rogers died of old age on 11 January 1967. This image highlights an interesting difference between British and French operated Nieuport 24s, with the British retaining the overwing-mounted Lewis gun, while the French opted for a nose-mounted Vickers gun, synchronised to fire through the propeller arc. (Canadian Armed Forces)

Above A revealing view of the nose section and twin .303-inch Vickers gun installation of a **Sopwith Snipe Ia**, or Long Range Snipe, meant to serve as a long range escort with the RAF's Independent Force. The tank immediately below the guns holds lubricating oil, something that rotary engines consumed in fairly liberal quantities. The lower tank carries the aircraft's fuel, the pilot sitting atop this 50 imperial gallon capacity tank, increased from the 32 imperial gallons of the standard Snipe. Apparently, the extra weight associated with the structural changes required, including 'beefing up' the front, inner interplane struts and introducing modest sweepback to the wings, was such as to rob the fighter of much of its agility. (Hawker)

Below Although essentially too late to take part in wartime combat, the light and small design approach adopted by Rex Pierson in producing the **Vickers Vimy** makes an interesting comparision with the larger, earlier Handley Page 0/100 and 0/400 series of bombers and also goes to illustrate just how long a gestation time is required between drawing board and production even in times of war. Seen here is the fourth and last of the Vimy prototypes, serial no F 9569 and the first of the machines to use the 360hp Rolls-Royce Eagle VIII, the engine selected to power subsequent production aircraft. Originating in design terms from around July 1917, the first of the Vimys made its maiden flight on 30 November 1917. Once the Eagle VIII had been adopted, the three man Vimy bomber was seen to have a top level speed of 106.5mph at 3,000 feet, an endurance of 11 hours and be capable of lifting a maximum bomb load of 2,476lb. While no less than 1,130 Vimys had been ordered at the time of the Armistice, only 13 had been completed, of which only one had been dispatched to Nancy in France for operational evaluation by the RAF's Independent Force. In the wake of the war's end, Vimy orders were cut back to 112 aircraft. (Rolls-Royce)

Above, right **William Wendell Rogers** in the cockpit of his No 1 Squadron, RFC, Nieuport 24, shortly after joining the unit in the spring of 1917. Rogers was to stay with No 1 Squadron throughout the remainder of the war. Born on Canada's east-

The Nelson Touch

Mention has already been made both in the preface and Chapter 1 of the Admiralty's far more pragmatic approach to the exploitation of aviation in naval warfare, compared with the attitudes prevalent in the War Office. Certainly, right from the outset of British military aviation endeavours, it was the Royal Navy who showed the greater initiative by putting aircraft aboard ships and doing the occasional pre-war experiment with arming aircraft. Compare this with the very firm War Office disapproval passed down to a young Capt. H.R.M. Brooke-Popham, who, having taken command of No 2 (Aeroplane) Company, RFC, in late April 1912, had the temerity to take a rifle and later a

machine gun aloft aboard a Bleriot IXM. Add this difference in mind-set to the money-driven underlying rivalries that pre-existed between these two rather austere offices of equally entrenched and often opposed opinion and it is not so surprising to see why, on 1 July 1914, the Admiralty saw fit to take back full control of the naval wing of the Royal Flying Corps.

In the light of what the Royal Naval Air Service achieved during the 43 wartime months of its existence, prior to its absorption into the newly created Royal Air Force on 1 April 1918, it is, perhaps, just as well that the two services operated with the degree of policy independence they did.

That these long standing rivalries between the Admiralty and War Office continued into the period of the war itself should come as no surprise. It was shown time and time again by the intransigence of one or the other over the allocation of material resources, whether they be aero-engines or boot laces. But what these frequently tedious, sometimes protracted petty arguments should not be allowed to hide is the very real operational collaboration that was seen to exist between the RNAS and the RFC units at moments of crisis. The 'we're all in this together' attitude is nowhere better exemplified than in the case of the Sopwith Triplane-equipped Naval 10's contribution to the hard-pressed RFC units' efforts during the Battle of Arras in mid-1917.

The one other matter the author feels compelled to comment upon is the sheer indomitability of a mere handful of people, who collectively shaped the RNAS into one of the finest bodies of men to take up arms on behalf of their country. Some of this small band figure prominently in the pages that follow, men such as Charles Rumney Samson; but there were also those such as Murray F. Sueter, whose behind-the-scenes efforts did so much to create the aeroplanes and weapons with which the RNAS went to war.

Below This image of a **Sopwith 1½ Strutter** being flown from a makeshift turret-top platform epitomises the initiative and invention so often displayed by the Royal Navy and its Air Service during World War I. The Royal Naval Air Service's innate sense of 'daring do' is exemplified in many ways, ranging from tackling Zeppelins in their lairs to developing Britain's first heavy bombers, and provides quite a contrast with the much more restricted thinking of those charged with shaping the development of the Royal Flying Corps. (Hawker)

Below **Charles Rumney Samson**, born in 1883, came to epitomise the pugnacious spirit of early British naval aviation. Samson entered the Royal Naval College, Greenwich, as a cadet in 1898 and left as a sub-lieutenant in 1904. On 4 April 1910, Samson received the Aero Club Aviator's Certificate No 71 and from this time on, for the next eight years, Samson's destiny was bound up with naval aviation and its development. Samson, a born leader of men, remained an active pilot throughout this period, some of the highlights of which included his making the world's second only take-off from a warship, on 10 January 1912, and then in May 1918, when nearly losing his life attempting to fly the unforgiving Sopwith Camel from off a destroyer-towed lighter. Although destined never to down an enemy in combat, Samson's disciplined aggression was to have a profound impact on his foes, wherever he and his men where to go. Samson was in command of the RNAS's Eastchurch Wing at the start of the war, from where he moved the unit to its new base at Ostend within a matter of weeks. It was from here that Samson and his unit fought a valiant series of harrying actions against the might of the German army, using both his aeroplanes and the world's first fleet of improvised armoured cars, assembled and converted with the help of his brother Felix. From here on through the ill-fated Gallipoli Campaign of 1915 and his continuing 1916 Middle East forays with the seaplane tender, HMS *Ben-My-Chree*, Samson's resolve never flagged. From May 1917 and back in Britain, the indefatigable Samson turned his mind to countering the dual threat of Zeppelins and U-boats. Absorbed into the newly formed RAF from April 1918, with the rank of Lieutenant Colonel, Samson was given command of No 4 Group, precursor of RAF Coastal Command. Samson retired from the RAF in 1929 as an Air Commodore. Samson is seen here in the cockpit of a Nieuport 10, while operating from the island of Tenedos in the Aegean Sea during 1915. (Cowin Collection)

Opposite, top and centre The **Sopwith Tabloid**, serial no 394 seen here, typifies the best of the RNAS's front-line equipment at the start of the war. Powered by a 100hp Gnome and capable of a top level speed of 92mph at sea level, the single seater was able to carry a couple of 20lb bombs and as such was to become the first British aircraft to fly a significant strike against German forces, when, on 8 October 1914, a bomb dropped from Lt R.L.G. Marix's Tabloid, serial no 168, destroyed the Zeppelin Z IX in its shed at Dusseldorf. The lower picture shows the once mighty Zeppelin Z IX's hulk smouldering in its lair following the daring raid by Marix. Flying his No 1 Naval Wing machine from an already embattled Antwerp, Marix's Tabloid was damaged during the attack, resulting in the pilot having to force land twenty miles short of his base, completing his journey by borrowed bicycle. Between April 1914 and May 1915, the RNAS took delivery of 39 Tabloids. (Hawker and Cowin Collection)

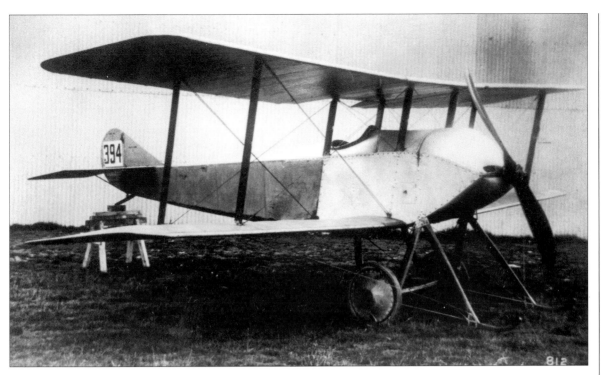

East Africa on 21 February 1915, where despite being adversely affected by the climate, they played a part in the ultimate destruction of the German cruiser, *Konigsberg*, on 11 July 1915. (Hawker)

Below Designed for reconnaissance duties, the two-seat **Sopwith Admiralty Type 807** seaplane emerged in 1914. Powered by a 100hp Gnome Monosoupape, the machine had a top level speed of 80mph at sea level. Serial no 807, seen here, was the first of these aircraft delivered to the RNAS, their serial nos being 807-810 and 919-926. Both 920 and 921 arrived in

Below Famed for teaching at least two generations of RAF pilots to fly, the Avro 504 had enjoyed a previous life as both a bomber and fighter during the first year of war, being used by both the RNAS and RFC. Seen here is one of forty **Avro 504B** two seaters that were produced, all going to the RNAS. Powered by either an 80hp Gnome or Le Rhone and with a top level speed of 82mph at sea level, some of these machines were known to have been flown operationally from the Dunkirk area, being used to raid Zeppelin sheds and submarine bases set up by the Germans further east along the coast. Just how the demand for military aircraft was to grow is demonstrated by the fact that prior to the large scale production of the Avro 504K trainer, the total RFC and RNAS orders placed for the type between 1914 and 1915 amounted to a mere 68 machines. (British Official/Crown Copyright)

Above The cockade on the rudder of this **Nieuport 10A.2** reconnaissance two seater, along with the uniforms of the attendant personnel positively identify it as belonging to an RFC unit, but the aircraft was also operated by the RNAS and it was this service that took a more muscular attitude in its deployment of the type, sometimes replacing the second seat with a .303-inch Lewis gun to give the machine a more agressive role. Powered by an 80hp Gnome or Le Rhone rotary, the top level speed was 90mph at sea level. The machine was used by France, both British services, the Italians, who also deployed it as a single-seat fighter, and Belgium

Below An early **Sopwith Baby**, or **Schneider**, fitted with a 100hp Gnome Monosoupape. The RNAS bought their first Babys shortly after the start of hostilities, using them as unarmed scouts. However, from early 1915 onwards these little

seaplanes were fitted with a swivellable-in-elevation-only, over-wing-mounted .303-inch Lewis gun and employed as armed shipboard scouts or for the local defence of seaplane bases. A little too fragile to operate in much of the weather experienced around Britain and the North Sea during winter, the Baby came into its own when operated in the Balkans and Middle East. Production of the type commenced in November 1914, with 296 being built. (British Official/Crown Copyright)

Above A revealing aspect on an experimental Lewis gun mounting on this late production **Sopwith Tabloid** scout. Note the armoured propeller cuffs approximately half way out along each blade, used to deflect any impacting round of ammunition. (Hawker)

machines were operated as single seaters. Total Type L build was put at just under 600 machines. (both British Official/Crown Copyright)

Above The **Morane-Saulnier BB** two seat reconnaissance and escort fighter biplane, if nothing else, typifies the paucity of Britain's own aircraft manufacturing capability during the earlier part of the war. Never operated by the French, the type was bought in early 1915 for use by both the RNAS and RFC. Powered by either an 80hp or 110hp Le Rhone rotary, the BB's top level speed with the higher powered engine was 91mph at sea level. As can be seen here, the BB carried two .303-inch Lewis guns, both being observer-operated. The joint service buy is reported to have been for not less than 28 aircraft, with two or three serving with No 4 Squadron, RNAS, while the RFC contingent served with their Nos 1, 3, 4 and 60 Squadrons. However, it should be noted that it was not until well into 1916 that Britain started to employ the one type of machine in a squadron, rather than a mix as previously. (British Official/Crown Copyright)

Above and below Considered something of a maverick by his commanding officers, Flt Sub Lt **Reginald Alexander John Warneford**, VC, was born on 15 October 1892 and qualified as a pilot on 25 February 1915. Warneford's name shot to prominence when, on 7 June 1915, he downed the German army's Zeppelin LZ 37 over Ghent in Belgium, while flying one of No 1 Wing, RNAS's Morane-Saulnier Type Ls from Furnes, east of Dunkirk. For this feat and reflecting the awe in which the Zeppelin was still held by the British, the young naval aviator was awarded Britain highest military honour, the Victoria Cross. Sadly, Warneford was to lose his own life, along with that of his passenger, a mere ten days later, on 17 June 1915, when he stalled and crashed while flying a Henry Farman. Also seen here is the actual **Morane-Saulnier Type L**, serial no 3253, used by Warneford to destroy LZ 37 by overflying it and dropping 20lb Hale bombs upon the dirigible. Powered by an 80hp Gnome or Le Rhone, the two seat Type L had a top level speed of 71mph at sea level. The Type L was operated by the French and the Russians, as well as the RNAS, who had bought 25, the delivery of which took place in early 1915. Many of the RNAS

Above From all reports, the cumbersome **Blackburn TB** was a real pilot frightener from the moment it first appeared in August 1915. Designed around the unsuccessful 150hp Smith radial, the two man TB was meant to serve as a long range, over-water Zeppelin destroyer. As if the failure of the Smith engine was not enough, leaving the TB underpowered it did, the airframe itself, left much to be desired in terms of structural bracing. During the 1916 flight trials, this weakness manifested itself not just in excessive drag, but, even more alarmingly, in a tendency for the outer wings to warp in opposition to aileron input from the pilot, making for ineffective roll control. Of the nine TBs built, eight ended up using twin 100hp Gnomes, while the final example, serial no 1517 seen here, had twin 110hp Clergets. Top level speed was a desultory 86mph at sea level and of the seven machines delivered and flown by the RNAS, none were put into operational service prior to the TB's early withdrawal from inventory. (Blackburn)

Above Serial no C 23, seen here, was one of 26 **C, or Coastal Class** non-rigid airships delivered to the RNAS commencing in September 1915. With an extremely useful endurance of 24 hours, the C Class was deployed around Britain's eastern and southern coastlines as a U-boat deterrent. With a crew of five, these trefoil sectioned craft were propelled by a 200hp tractor-propeller forward engine, plus a pusher propeller 100hp engine at the rear of the underslung crew gondola. Under this impetus, the C Class's top level speed at sea level was 50mph. (British Official/Crown Copyright)

Below and bottom While the designers and engineers at Handley Page must be given credit for building the finished product, the true creator of Britain's first long range, heavy bomber, the **Handley Page 0/100** was Murray F. Sueter, who, as Director

of the Admiralty's Air Department in late 1914, went to their Lordships with a request to develop a ' bloody paralyser' of an aeroplane initially envisaged as being capable of long range, over-water patrolling. This demand formally emerged from the Admiralty Air Department on 28 December 1914 and was taken up by Handley Page, who first flew their prototype 0/100 just under a year later, on 17 December 1915. Incidentally, this flight was made by Lt Cmdr J.T. Babington, RNAS, the Navy's on-site man responsible for nursing the 0/100 from its birth to its initial operational deployment in October 1916, with Babington then commanding the 'Handley Page' Squadron, attached to the RNAS's 3rd Wing, based near Nancy in eastern France. Unfortunately for the RNAS, initial deliveries were slow, coupled to which early 0/100 operations, commencing in November 1916, were off-shore patrols, usually carried out by single aircraft in daylight. However, all 0/100 missions were switched to night flights after one had been lost to enemy action over the North Sea, on the 25 April 1917. Indeed, the continuing use of 0/100s in ones and twos to raid German submarine and Gotha bases along the Belgium coast characterised operations during the first half of 1916 and its was not until mid-August 1917 that 0/100s began to be dispatched in two-digit strength. Capable of lifting a bomb load of up to 1,792lb, 40 of the 46 four man 0/100s built were powered by twin 250hp Rolls-Royce Eagle IIs, giving a top level speed of 76mph at sea level, while the last six machines used the 320hp Sunbeam Cossack that pushed the top level speed up to 84.5mph at sea level. The larger of the two images shows 0/100, serial no 3116, of the RNAS's 5th Wing based at Coudekerque, taken on 4 March 1917 and accompanied here by a Sopwith Triplane and a Nieuport 24bis. The smaller of the two photographs is of 0/100, serial no B 9446, the first of the six Sunbeam Cossack-powered machines that served as a bridging development between the 0/100 and the 0/400. (Philip Jarrett Collection and Handley Page)

Opposite, top The **Handley Page 0/400** was a direct development of the 0/100 employing twin 360hp Rolls Royce Eagle VIIIs or 400hp Liberty 12s for the planned US aircraft, the former engines giving the four-man bomber a top level speed of 97mph. The converted 0/100 that served as the prototype for the 0/400 was first flown in September 1917, but initial deliveries of the planned 400 aircraft did not start until March 1918,

the first going to No 16 Squadron, RNAS, just prior to their becoming No 216 Squadron, RAF, on 1 April 1918. The image of a 'folded' 0/400 seen here has been chosen specifically to emphasise some of the problems imposed on aircraft designers by the occasional need to hangar such large machines in something not much better than a king-sized tent. (Handley Page)

Below and right Today there are few that remember that the **Sopwith 1¹/₂ Strutter** started its life as the Sopwith **Type 9700** designed to meet an RNAS need for a two-seat reconnaissance fighter. With an Admiralty order for 150 aircraft in hand, Sopwiths completed the first example in mid-December 1915 and wasted little time in delivering initial production machines to operational RNAS units early in the new year of 1916. Powered by various 110hp to 130hp rotaries, the 1¹/₂ Strutter had a top level speed of 106mph at sea level, decreasing to 102mph at 6,500 feet. For armament, the machine used a fixed, forward-firing Vickers, plus a flexibly-mounted Lewis for the observer. Of the 550 aircraft delivered to the RNAS, around 130 were of the single-seat bomber variety, which could carry up to 300lb of weapons in the shape of twelve 25lb bombs, while the two seaters lifted 224lb, or four 56lb bombs.

The type's performance was such as to lead to orders not just from the RFC, but from several other nations and the machine's broader programme history is dealt with earlier in the chapter on French aircraft. The larger of the two images seen here is of serial no N5504, one of the single seat bombers and 4th of a 50 aircraft Sopwith-built batch for the RNAS. The smaller image is of an RNAS 1¹/₂ Strutter departing from atop one of a capital warship's main turrets. This kind of operation was to become relatively routine from April 1918 onwards. (both Hawker)

Above An Australian, born the son of a blacksmith in 1889, **Harry George Hawker** quit school at the age of twelve to become a motor mechanic. By the age of fifteen, he was making good money as a chauffeur/mechanic. With £100 savings in his pocket, the slight, rather frail looking Hawker joined a group of other young Australians heading for England in early 1911. In setting out for England, Hawker had hoped to quickly earn enough to gain his pilot's certificate. However, for well over a year after his arrival, Hawker's fortunes languished to the point where he was contemplating his return home. His luck was to change in June 1912, when he was recommended to Sopwith's engineer by Harry Kauper, one of Hawker's travelling companions on the trip from home. Before month's end, Hawker was on the company's pay roll as a mechanic, opting in August 1912 to spend the last £40 of his savings on taking flying lessons. The first fruit of this investment came on 17 September 1912, when Hawker, who had proved to be a natural flier, received his aviator's certificate. Just over a month later, on 24 October 1912, Hawker had established a new British endurance record of 8 hours 23 minutes flying a Sopwith Wright. Within a further year, Hawker was not only the holder of the British flying records for speed, altitude and endurance, he was already beginning to provide vital inputs to the Sopwith design team, starting with the diminutive Sopwith Tabloid. From this time onwards, Hawker was not just responsible for flight testing all of Sopwith's machines, but materially influenced their design, including that of the 1½ Strutter, the Pup, the Triplane and the Camel. Equally at home in a racing car or an aeroplane, Harry Hawker died of his injuries on 12 July 1921, following a crash while practicing for that year's Aerial Derby in the British Nieuport Goshawk. (Hawker)

Below Loved by those that flew it, the graceful single seat fighter that everyone has come to know as the **Sopwith Pup** was produced to another of those far-sighted Admiralty requirements, known as the **Sopwith Type 9901**. First flown during the spring of 1916, the Pup went to France for operational evaluation by RNAS pilots in May 1916, where it was universally acclaimed for its speed and agility. On the basis of this acclaim, both the Admiralty and the War Office placed large orders for the type, with No 8 Squadron of No 1 Wing, RNAS, receiving the first six production deliveries in late October 1916. The first RFC unit to equip with the Pup was No 54 Squadron, who brought their machines to France on 24 December 1916. Powered by various rotaries of 80hp to 100hp, the Pup was armed with a single, fixed, synchronised .303-inch Vickers. Top level speed of the Pup was 111.5mph at sea level, falling off to 102mph at 10,000 feet. The Pup could climb to 5,000 feet in 5 minutes 20 seconds and 10,000 feet in 14 minutes, while the aircraft's ceiling was 18,500 feet. Used to devastating effect during the Battle of Arras in the spring of 1917, such was the pace of advance in fighter development that the Pup had been rendered obsolescent in front-line terms by the late summer of 1917. Although rapidly supplanted by the Sopwith Triplane in front-line RNAS service, the Pup continued to serve with home defence squadrons, while a RNAS Pup, flown by Flt Sub-Lt B.A. Smart from the cruiser HMS *Yarmouth* was responsible for the downing of naval Zeppelin L 23, on1 August 1917. Total Pup build is cited as exceeding 1,800 aircraft when production ended in the autumn of 1918. Pup, serial no A 7302 seen here happens to be the 2nd of 50 late production aircraft built by the Standard Motor Company for the RFC. (Hawker)

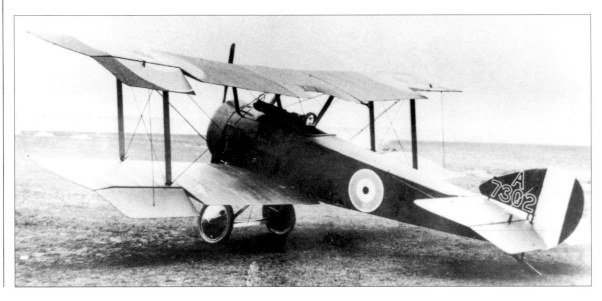

Below Born in British Columbia, Canada, on 22 November 1893, **Raymond Collishaw**, while still in his 'teens had seen more of the world than most ever would, thanks to holding a maritime Second Mates Ticket. In January 1916, Collishaw travelled to Britain at his own expense to join the RNAS as a trainee pilot. Subsequently, his operational baptism came flying Sopwith 1 1/2 Strutters with No 3 Wing, RNAS. It was with this unit that Collishaw scored his first two victories, both on 25 October 1916, prior to surviving being downed himself on 27 December 1916. Collishaw's next move was to Sopwith Pup-equipped No 3 Squadron, RNAS, on 1 February 1917. Between then and 10 April, when he left to join No 10 Squadron, RNAS, as a flight commander, Collishaw added a further two 'kills' to his tally. It was with 'Naval 10' flying the new Sopwith Triplane that Collishaw gathered four fellow Canadians around him and set

about 'cutting their teeth' on German aircraft operating in the Ostend area. On 30 May 1917 the squadron moved south to aid hard pressed RFC units engaged in the air war above the Battle of Arras. Between 1 June 1917 and 27 July 1917, Collishaw's score of confirmed victories climbed from 9 to 38, while his companions on 'Naval 10' were equally busy at the business of turning the Triplane into a legend. Withdrawn from combat for a while. Collishaw converted to Sopwith Camels and between 10 December 1917 and 26 September 1918 extended his tally by another 21 'kills' to take his pre-Armistice total to 59. For most of this time, Collishaw was in command of 'Naval 3', or No 203 Squadron, RAF, after 1 April 1918. Collishaw went on to command No 201 Group in North Africa, prior to heading No 12 Group. Fighter Command during World War II, retiring in 1943 as an Air Vice Marshal. Incidentally, all but five of this stalwart Canadian's victories were fighters. (Public Archives Canada)

Below The story of one of Britain's finest fighters is one of nothing less than a glorious opportunity carelessly thrown away. The first of the Admiralty-funded **Sopwith Triplane** single-seat fighters , serial no N500, was completed on 28 May 1916, with Harry Hawker giving it its first air test that day. Such was the Australian's confidence in the machine that he is reported to have looped the aircraft within three minutes of its first lift-off. By mid-June 1916 the machine was in northern France, being put through its operational evaluation by RNAS pilots, who all were particularly impressed by its phenomenal rate of climb. The tone of the ensuing report was extremely complimentary to the point that, as in the case of the preceding Pup, the Triplane was ordered into large scale production for both the RNAS and RFC. All of these events, it should be noted occurred before the end of summer 1916. Then, on 30 September 1916, in a letter to the War Office, Sir Douglas Haig warned that British air superiority over the Somme was in serious jeopardy thanks to the emergence of the new German fighters. Haig followed this first letter within a matter of weeks by asking for an extra twenty fighter squadrons. This should have given even

more impetus to the gathering Triplane programme, but for reasons far more to do with the convoluted political machinations of Whitehall than the rational allocation of resources, the earlier large RFC order for the demonstrably useful Triplane appears to evaporate, while even the RNAS allocation becomes limited to 150 aircraft. Further, all this prevarication held Sopwiths back in terms of delivering production machines, these failing to appear much before year-end 1916. The part played by the Triplane in support of the beleaguered RFC squadrons has already been touched upon in the preceding entry on Raymond Collishaw, as indeed was the Triplane's impact on the Germans, dealt with in the earlier, companion volume to this work. Certainly, it would seem that during this period, the Germans gained considerable help from Whitehall! The vast majority of Triplanes were powered by the 130hp Clerget, giving the machine a top level speed of 117mph at 5,000 feet, decreasing to 105mph at 15,000 feet. The Triplane's ceiling was 20,000 feet, while it took 6 minutes 20 seconds to reach 6,500 feet and 10 minutes 35 seconds to achieve 15,000 feet. The standard Triplane armament consisted of a single, synchronised .303-inch Vickers gun. (Hawker)

Below The Short Brothers Company, established in November 1908, had enjoyed a long standing good relationship with the Admiralty's Air Department and especially with its visionary head, Murray F Sueter. Between 1912 and 1914, Shorts had developed a series of tractor-engined seaplanes, culminating in the first of the so-called Short 'Folders', of which the Admiralty had bought 25. Thus, at the outbreak of war in early August 1914, Shorts were already established as the leading supplier of naval seaplanes in Britain. These early seaplanes, one of which had been the first British aircraft to loft and drop a torpedo on 27 July 1914, were followed by the Short Admiralty Type 166 and other small run series precursors to the seemingly ubiquitously built and deployed, torpedo-carrying **Short Admiralty Type 184** that emerged in the spring of 1915. More than 650 of these two seaters were to be produced by Shorts and 10

sub-contractors. Incidentally, the first Type 184s to be deployed served aboard HMS *Ben-My-Cree* from June 1915. Indeed, the Type 184 was the first ever aircraft to sink a ship by torpedo, on 17 August 1915, albeit that the ship in question was a tug boat attacked while the aircraft was taxiing in the Aegean Sea, where the high temperatures reduced performance considerably. Aware of this grave limitation, Sueter sought solutions via two routes, the first being to contract for the design of twin-engined types such as the Blackburn GP, dealt with below, while beseeching sympathetic engine suppliers to produce a power unit with sufficient output to make a single-engined torpedo-carrier a real possibility. In the case of Shorts, it was the emergence of an engine adequate to the task that did the trick, leading to their two-seat **Short Admiralty Type 310**, a more powerful development of the Type 184. First flown in July 1916 and powered by the 320hp Sunbeam Cossack, the Type 310 could carry a 1,000lb, 18 inch torpedo when cruising at around 68mph, while the top level speed at sea level, without torpedo was 79mph. Ironically, by the time the Type 310 was ready for service use its primary role had been given over to carrier-based landplane types, such as the Sopwith Cuckoo, with the result that the Short seaplane's mission was switched to over-water patrolling. Seen here is serial no N1303, the 14th Type 310 to be built by Shorts, who, incidentally, were to supply six of these machines to the Japanese Navy at the end of 1917. (Shorts)

Opposite, top left Only two examples of the three-seat **Blackburn GP** long range patrol and torpedo bomber were built, the first being completed in July 1916. These two contemporaries and rivals to the Short Type 310 differed in both structural detail and the type of engine employed. The first example, serial no 1415 seen here, used twin 150hp Sunbeam Nubians, while serial no 1416, which did not emerge until near the close of 1916, was powered by twin 190hp Rolls-Royce Falcons. The top level speed of the latter floatplane was 97mph at sea level, its ceiling 11,000 feet and climb to 5,000 feet took

10 minutes. Armament comprised two flexibly-mounted .303-inch Lewis guns, plus a 14-inch torpedo, or four 230lb bombs. The Admiralty elected not to proceed with further development, but a landplane version, powered by twin 270hp Rolls-Royce Falcon IIIs and known as the **Blackburn Kangaroo** was subsequently produced for the RFC, who took 20 examples. (Blackburn)

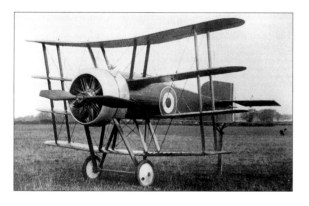

Above and below The **Fairey Campania**, named after His Majesty's seaplane carrier for which it was built to operate, started life as the Fairey F 16 of 1916 and via the sole F 17 entered production in early 1917. A two-seat carrier-borne reconnaissance or coastal patroller, 37 of the 62 Campanias built used various marks of Roll-Royce Eagles with outputs of between 250hp and 345hp, while the other 25 machines were powered by the 260hp Sunbeam Maori II. As the world's first carrier-going design, the machine was mounted on a wheeled trolley for take-off from the vessel's 200-feet long flight deck, the trolley being dropped and retrieved for subsequent use. On returning to its floating mobile base, the aircraft would alight on the water beside the ship from where it would be hoisted back aboard. Top level speed was typically 89mph at sea level, dropping to 78mph at 6,500 feet. Armament comprised a single flexibly-mounted .303-inch Lewis gun, plus light bombs carried under the centre section. The top image depicts the first Campania, serial no N 1000, unique in having a small fin and engine exhausts that went up through the upper wing leading edge. The image below shows the 5th aircraft, serial no N1004 in its wings folded configuration. (both Fairey)

Above For every new type that enters service there are usually at least two rival designs that failed to make it. One such was the sole, single-seat **Wight Quadruplane** fighter, completed in August 1916. No doubt designed in the belief that if adding a third wing to the Sopwith Pup can have such a beneficial effect, a fourth should do wonders! Sadly this was not to be so with this machine, serial no N546, seen here in its interim, early 1917 form. Following trials that extended into July 1917, the Admiralty lost interest in this 110hp Clerget-engined machine. (British Official/Crown Copyright)

Left Designed as a side-by-side, two seat flying boat trainer, 179 examples of the **Norman Thompson NT 2B** are known to have been built of the 284 ordered. Derived from the sole NT 2A tandem seat flying boat fighter, the NT 2Bs used either the 150hp or 200hp Hispano-Suiza, or the derivative Sunbeam Arab. Deliveries of the NT 2B commenced in December 1917, the type being flown in large numbers from Calshot and Lee-on-Sea on the south coast, while more were based at Felixstow on the east coast. Top level speed of the NT 2B was typically 85mph at 2,000 feet, while its ceiling was 11,400 feet. Serial no N2560 seen here was from the last production batch of 25 aircraft to be completed. Note the enclosed cockpit. (British Official/Crown Copyright)

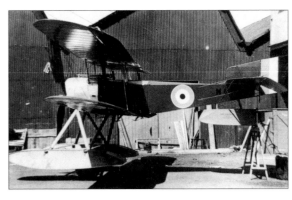

Above and below If the above mentioned Fairey Campania was the world's first dedicated carrier-going aircraft design, the **Sopwith T 1 Cuckoo** set the mould for all subsequent carrier-borne machines by adopting wheels in place of floats. First flown in June 1917, the Cuckoo used a 200hp Sunbeam Arab and production deliveries of this single-seat torpedo bomber did not get underway for over a year, thanks in large part to the fact that the Admiralty were still experimenting with the flight deck layout of HMS *Furious*, while awaiting the September 1918 completion of HMS *Argus*. Because time concerns were not as pressing as normal, the Admiralty also elected to have the aircraft built by sub-contractors, rather than by Sopwith themselves. As it was, the first production deliveries were made to the Torpedo Aeroplane School at East Fortune in Scotland during early August 1918, with the first carrier-going deliveries being made to No 210 Squadron, RAF, aboard HMS *Argus* in late October 1918. Of the 260 Cuckoos ordered , just over 90 had been delivered at the time of the Armistice. Top level speed of the Cuckoo was 103.5mph at sea level, its ceiling being 12,100 feet. The Iimage seen here above shows serial no N6950, the first of 50 Blackburn-built aircraft dropping an 18 inch Mk IX torpedo. The picture below is of three Cuckoos aboard the aircraft carrier HMS *Furious*, with serial no N6980, a Blackburn-built aircraft nearest the camera. (both Hawker Siddeley Aviation)

Above Old soldiers never die and neither it seems do good aircraft designs, as evidenced by the 1916 **Fairey Hamble Baby** resurrection of the little Sopwith floatplanes sired by the 1914 Schneider Tabloid. In essence, the Hamble Baby was little more than the earlier Sopwith Baby except in one respect. The difference lay in the use of the Fairey Camber Changing gear, which in effect was a system of right and left side, half span trailing edge flaps that could be made to work in unison for increased lift, or differentially for lateral, or roll control. Incidentally, this system, which allowed the machine to fly with higher loads than previously possible, was to be employed on every subsequent Fairey biplane up to and including their Swordfish. The first of the Fairey machines completed prior to the end of 1916 was, in fact, a converted Sopwith Baby, this being followed six months later by the first production Hamble Babys, these going into service as single-seat anti-submarine patrollers during the summer of 1917. Powered by either a 110hp or 130hp Clerget, the Hamble Baby had a top speed of 90mph at 2,000 feet to which height it could climb in 5 minutes 30 seconds. Its defensive armament comprised a single, synchronised Lewis gun, while its offensive warload was two underslung 65lb bombs. As was often the case, Faireys themselves only produced 50 of the total 180 examples built, the 130 lion's share coming from sub-contractor Parnall & Sons, Bristol. (Fairey)

Above and right Built at their Barrow-in-Furness facility, the **Vickers R 23** was the first quasi-operational British airship and the lead machine of four, then two improved class of dirigibles. Powered by four 250hp Rolls-Royce Eagles, the 17 man crew R 23 had a top level speed of 52mph and cruised at 40mph. Short on bouyancy, the R 23's ceiling was an alarmingly low 3,000 feet, whilst its maximum bomb load of 400lb was around a ninth that of its near contemporary, the Imperial German Navy's 'u' class, L 48. First flown in September 1917, the R23 was delivered to the RNAS Airship Station at Pulham in Norfolk on the 15th of that month. Subsequently mainly employed on training duties, the R 23 was adopted as a mother ship for two Sopwith Camels during the summer of 1918. The other airships in this class consisted of the Beardmore-built R 24, Armstrong Whitworth's R 25 and the Vickers-built R 26. The two R23X or Improved R 23 Class airships were Beardmore's R 27 and Armstrong Whitworth's R 29. The larger of the images above shows R 23 being 'walked' at Pulham, while the smaller right depicts Sopwith 2F Camel, serial no N6814, of No 212 Squadron, RAF, slung from beneath R 23 at Pulham. The second Camel used in these trials was serial no 6622 and came from the same squadron. While the first release from R 23 involved an unmanned Camel with locked controls, at least one 'live' release was made, with Lt R.E. Keys landing the Camel back at Pulham. (both Vickers)

All this page A development of the earlier IF Camel, the **Sopwith 2F Camel** was evolved specifically for naval use, being characterised by its shorter wingspan and detachable rear fuselage to facilitate shipboard storage. Powered by either a 150hp Bentley BR 1, the standard engine, or a 130hp Clerget 9B, the first 2F Camel was completed and flying by March 1917, however, it then took around six months before production deliveries began to flow to the service users. Developed specifically as a Zeppelin killer, the 2F Camel had a top level speed of 122mph at 10,000 feet, decreasing to 117mph at 15,000 feet. Its time to climb to 10,000 feet was 11 minutes 30 seconds,

increasing to 25 minutes to reach 15,000 feet, while its ceiling was 17,300 feet. The machine's armament consisted of a nose-mounted Vickers, along with an overwing Lewis gun, while two 50lb bombs could be slung below the centre section. The 2F Camel was deployed in depth around the North Sea and on both sides of the English Channel; they were carried about and launched from atop battleship and battle cruiser main turrets, they were put aboard the Royal Navy's first aircraft carriers, while more venturesome minds, such as that of Charles Rumney Samson, conceived the idea of launching them from lighters, towed at high speed by destroyers. That they achieved the task set them is attested to by the fact that they account-

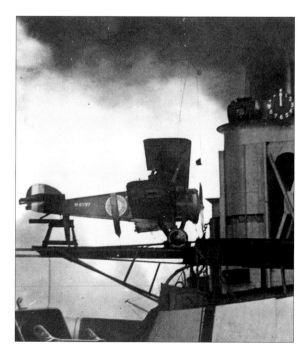

ed for three Zeppelins, L 54 and L 60 being destroyed at their Trondern base by seven 2F Camel bombers, launched from HMS *Furious* on 17 July 1918, while less than a month later, L 53 was brought down by Lt S.D. Culley, RN, from a towed lighter launch on 11 August 1918. Perhaps the most surprising thing about the 2F Camel saga was the fact that there were relatively so few of them produced, with Sopwith building 50, backed by Beardmore, who assembled a further 100 machines. The first of the four images used here shows a frontal aspect on the prototype 2F Camel, serial no N5, followed by a complimentary view, taken from the rear of serial no N 7136, one of the Beardmore built fighters. The picture bottom left is of Lt S.D. Culley, RN, during the first successful tow lighter demonstration, made on 31 July 1918. Here it should be recalled that Cdr Samson had nearly lost his life attempting this feat some weeks earlier, when his Camel snagged some ties during launch. The final picture is of serial no N 6797 on its launching platform atop 'X' turret of the battle cruiser, HMS *Tiger*. (first two Hawker, second two British Official/Crown Copyright)

Below During 1916, Westlands, who were already a sub-contract aircraft builder for the Admiralty, was one of three firms that responded to an Admiralty requirement for a single

seat, shipboard, floatplane fighter whose performance should exceed a top level speed of 110mph and have a ceiling in excess of 20,000 feet. The company built two **Westland N 1Bs**, serial nos N 16 and N 17, both machines powered by a 150hp Bentley rotary. First flown during August 1917, the folding wing N 1B with its top level speed of 108mph at sea level was only marginally below the target figure. As it transpired the Admiralty floatplane fighter need was overtaken by the advent of the Sopwith 2F Camel. (Westland)

Below The writer makes no apology for including this less than perfect view of the one-off **Alcock A 1**, whose genesis encapsulated the truly remarkable spirit and initiative of some RNAS fliers. Designed and built on the Aegean island of Mudros by RNAS pilot John Alcock, presumably as a spare time venture, the single-seat fighter made use of some existing Sopwith components, as both Pups and Triplanes had operated from the island. However, it was what Alcock did with these that was so impressive, building them into an intelligently conceived airframe that was just about as robust as it could be, while providing the pilot with optimum visibility. Powered by a 110hp Clerget 9Z, the double bay, sesquiplane machine was armed with a single, synchronised .303-inch Vickers gun. Described by witnesses as being fast and agile, it is a great pity that no actual performance figures survive. Flown by one or two RNAS pilots on Mudros and Stavros, the A 1 reportedly made its maiden flight on 15 October 1917. A very real tragedy was that Alcock himself had been forced down and taken prisoner on 30 September 1917, only a fortnight prior to the aircraft's first flight. As to the fate of the A 1, sadly, it was ultimately to be 'written-off' as being beyond economic repair following a local crash. John Alcock was of course the same pilot who, when accompanied by navigator Arthur Whitten-Brown in a Vickers Vimy, was to win a lasting place in aviation's annals by making the first ever non-stop transatlantic crossing by aeroplane in mid-1919. (J.M. Bruce Collection)

Other Allies' Contributions

Besides the United States of America, whose entry into the war in April 1917 swung the material balance of the conflict solidly in the Allied nations' favour, there were only two other Allied countries with the capability to contribute much to the course of the 1914-1918 air war, Russia and Italy. Both not only had significantly sized air arms, but both also had a home-based industrial capability to help sustain their fliers.

As pointed out in the preamble to Chapter 1, Russia, with some 244 aeroplane and 12 airships, went to war with a larger number of military and naval aircraft than Britain could muster. As to the size of Russia's aircraft industry, this was smaller than those of either France or Germany, but was, again, larger than that of Britain at the time. These comparisions, however, only reveal part of the overall situation and to better understand Russia's strengths and weaknesses, it is necessary to make some qualitative judgements.

For many centuries before World War I, Russia's real strength had lain in its people and their stoicism in the face of adversity. To state the obvious, Russia's problems, as events would soon reveal, lay with its ruling establishment and their arrogant eliteist attitudes. Even without the onset of war, Russia's social structure was beginning to creak under the growing stresses being imposed upon it, largely from an aristocracy oblivious to any warning signs, including the battleship Potemkin and Odessa revolts of 1905. The coming of war could only increase the unrest.

Not surprisingly, the Imperial Russian Air Service and its smaller brother service, the naval air arm simply mirrored the larger problems facing the Russian people overall. Both services, organised and managed by an elite, but not necessarily effective officer corps, lacked adequate upward communication from enlisted men to their officers and, consequently, would often find themselves floundering in either an operational or logistical nightmare largely of their own making. In a more technical environment such as aviation, these shortfalls showed up as having far too many different types of aircraft on inventory, along with a minefield of difficulties when is came to locating and obtaining the necessary spare parts. Russian pilots were classed as being above the average when it came to bravery. Be that as it may, the job of flying a four-engined Sikorsky Ilya Mourometz fitted with a mix of differing engines was a daunting enough task brave or not, and apparently, this was frequently the situation facing Russian pilots simply as a result of breakdowns in the spare parts supply chain. Bravery is a poor substitute for organisation and faced with such a disciplined foe as the Germans it was inevitable that the Russian military could only collapse. Just how complete and demoralising this collapse was, when it came in the summer of 1917, is somewhat obscured by the Bolshevik Revolution of October 1917; an event that succeeded in totally removing Russia from the war.

Turning to Russia's aircraft industry of the period, this was already beginning to polarise around a small number of large manufacturers, making the contrast with Britain's industry even more marked, the Russian problem being a paucity of indigenous design capability. Thus, for the most part, the Russian aircraft industry appeared content to build other peoples' aeroplanes and in particular, those of French origin.

The young Igor Sikorsky was the one shining exception to this lack of 'home-spun' talent and by mid-1914 was already making a name for himself developing of a series of machines that were large to start with and got ever larger and more powerful as they progressed. These large Sikorskys, used as bombers, were in essence Russia's only major aeronautical contribution, for despite various attempts to produce indigenous Russian fighters, including two by Sikorsky, these were generally mediocre, forcing Russia to continue down the licence-built path. One really telling indicator of Russia's inability to properly gear itself up for war is the fact that whereas France, Germany and Britain had stepped up aircraft production and, hence, air force strengths by more than an order of magnitude by the end of 1916, the strength of the Russian air arms had only risen to 724 machines at this time – less than a threefold increase

Italy was in the fortunate position of being able to hold off entering the war for around nine months after most of the northwestern European nations were fully embroiled.

Further, largely geographically insulated from the major centre of German military activity far to the northwest, the Italian faced a relatively weak Austro-Hungarian opposition, whose main military effort was concentrated on the Eastern Front.

Thus, for more than two and a quarter years, Italy's war was confined to skirmishes with Austro-Hungarian forces on or around today's borders of Austria and Slovenia. However, the establishment of the Hindenberg Line and the collapse of Russia as a fighting entity in the summer of 1917 relieved the German High Command of much of the previous need to concentrate on the Western Front. As a result, in September 1917, the Germans were able to dispatch men and artillery to stiffen the Austro-Hungarians on the Italian Front.

At this time, Italy had fifteen relatively well equipped fighter squadrons, using Nieuport 17s, SPAD VIIs or Hanriot HD-1s, to defend their frontal airspace. If they had problems they were organisational to the extent that the air service elements were tied to a given Army Group. The implication of this was that it was far more difficult to muster fighter resources, in particular, at some crucial point, as the French, Germans and British had already learnt to do. Coupled to which, the Italian air arm's reconnaissance units were extremely vulnerable, being still reliant on obsolescent or obsolete Caudron G IVs or Savoia-Pomilio SP 2s. When the combined Austro-Hungarian and German assault came in late October 1917, its effect was overwhelming, forcing an Italian retreat back a distance of around 40 miles westwards along the coastal strip to the Piave River.

Here, the German-led thrust was halted, with the help of hastily organised support of British and French contingents, including air elements.

While stabilised at the Piave, fighting in this sector was to continue until the autumn of 1918, when, with the effective withdrawal of the German elements, the unsupported Austro-Hungarian effort effectively collapsed a few days prior to the Armistice. It was during this campaign that the series of large Caproni triplane and biplane bombers were operationally deployed. The fact that their effect was negligible was much more an indictment of the way they were deployed than of the efficacy of the machines or their crews.

Below Besides being used extensively by both the French and British forces, the **Nieuport 11** was to provide the backbone of other Allied nations' fighter forces, including those of Belgium, Italy and Russia. Shown here is an Italian unit equipped with the type, which served as Italy's standard fighter from its initial deployment with them during the summer of 1916 to mid-1917. In the case of Italy, the Nieuport 11's role extended beyond its operational use, as 450 of these machines were produced under licence in Italy by Nieuport-Macchi. Thus, it could be said that this nimble little machine not only helped secure Italian skies, but played no small part in helping establish the country's future aeronautical industrial base. (Cowin Collection)

Above The brainchild of Igor Sikorsky, who in later years and on another continent was to help pioneer the first of the practical helicopters, the four engined **Sikorsky Ilya Mourometz** was, without question, the world's first long range heavy bomber. Around 80 of these impressive craft had been completed by the time Russia withdrew from the war. Progressively re-engined from the original 100hp Argus to the 220hp Renault versions, the first ten bomber versions of the Ilya Mourometz were ordered in the spring of 1914, their initial deployment following in February 1915, this after the whole programme had nearly been abandoned. These machines, along with the men that crewed and maintained them, had been preserved as a group by M.V. Shidlovski, who, virtually single-handedly, created the world's first coherent bomber force, appointing himself its commander with the rank of Major General in the process. In reality, the Ilya Mourometz's were an evolving family of aircraft, of which only the basic layout remained unchanged. Even the later 220hp engined version of the Sikorsky bomber could only manage a top level speed of 85mph at 6,500 feet, while its operational ceiling was 10,500 feet. Capable of lifting a bomb load of 1,120lb, these machines were initially crewed by six men, with the later variants carrying seven. Similarly, defensive armament climbed from two to seven machine guns and they were clearly effective, as only one of the 73 known operational machines was to be brought down, this on 12 September 1916, after it had accounted for three enemy machines, plus a fourth damaged of the original seven attacking fighters. Apparently, this family of aircraft were extremely nose-heavy in the landing phase, so both pilots needed to be very muscular in applying back pressure to the elevator, while the rest of the crew were required to beat a hasty retreat into the machine's nether regions astern! (Cowin Collection)

Right The young **Alexander Prokofieff de Seversky**, seen here immediately after completing his first solo flight, on a Farman, at the School of Military Aviation, Sevastopol, in the spring of 1915. Born in 1894, de Seversky had graduated from the Imperial Russian Naval Academy in 1914 before learning to fly. Having gained his 'wings', de Seversky joined a naval bomber squadron operating in the eastern Baltic area. It was while operating with this unit, on 2 July 1915, that de Seversky was to lose a leg when his aircraft was shot down and a bomb it was carrying exploded. Undeterred, de Seversky, now with an artificial limb, went back to flying in the summer of 1916, this time in FBA Type C fighter flying boats. In these machines, de Seversky scored a confirmed 13 victories, making him Russia's third highest ranking air ace. Fortunately, Major de Seversky was in America, as part of the Imperial Russian Naval Air Mission at the time of Russia's internal collapse in the summer of 1917. It was here that de Seversky chose to remain in the wake of the October 1917 Revolution. As a friend and advisor to Brigadier General 'Billy' Mitchell, de Seversky developed one of the earlier automatic bomb sights during the 1920s, prior to

founding the Seversky Aircraft Corporation in 1931, Here, he specialised in producing, test flying and selling a line of fast mainly military monoplanes, leading to the US Army's 1937 P-35 fighter. Still cutting a dashing figure, de Seversky parted ways with the company he had set up at the start of the 1940s, becoming a consultant and author of the prophetic 1942 book 'Victory Through Air Power', while his former business venture became Republic Aviation, going on to produce the P-47 Thunderbolt and a series of jet fighters leading to the F-105 Thunderchief of 1959. As for this larger-than-life man , he passed away at the age of 80, in 1974. (de Seversky)

Below The prototype single seat **Sikorsky S.20**, serial no 267, is seen here with the insignia of the Imperial Russian Air Service on its rudder. Designed at the close of 1916, the S.20 was the victim of double misfortune in being underpowered and emerging just a few short months before Russia was to sue for peace as part of its political collapse in the spring of 1917. Two S.20s were built, the first using an 80hp Le Rhone, while the second machine had a 110hp Le Rhone. Top level speed of the higher powered S.20 was cited at 118mph, while it took 6 minutes 20 seconds to reach 6,540 feet. Its armament was to have been a single .303-inch Vickers, putting it at a disadvantage compared with contemporary foes. (Sikorsky)

Below An Italian operated **Voisin LA**, the machine being licence-built by SIT in substantial quantities throughout late 1915 and 1916. This particular aircraft used a 190hp Isotta-Fraschini V 4B. These lumbering, pusher-engined reconnaissance machines proved easy prey for the Austro-Hungarian fighters. (Cowin Collection)

Above **Francesco Baracca**, born on 9 May 1888, had held a commission in the crack Royal Piedmont Cavalry since the age of nineteen, to which he added his military aviator's 'wings' in 1912. Too late to put his flying experience to use in the Italian-Turkish War of 1911-1912, Baracca spent the years between 1912 and 1915 as a touring flying instructor, going from one military airfield to another. Interspersed with these duties, Baracca was asked to fly and evaluate many of the new military aircraft being offered to the Italian Government. Baracca was with a Paris-based Italian military mission at the time Italy declared war on the Austro-Hungarian Empire, on 19 May 1915, shortly afterwards returning to Italy to join a Nieuport

10 squadron serving on the Udine Front. Baracca's first confirmed 'kill' took a long seven months to materialise and came in the wake of his transfer to the single seat Nieuport 11-equipped 70th squadriglia at the end of 1915. This first victory, on 7 April 1916, involved a two seat Austrian Aviatik. Following in the footsteps of such great fighter aces as James McCudden and Manfred von Richthofen, Baracca appears to have specialised in downing two seaters. In June 1917, Baracca, whose current score was 13, took command of the SPAD S VII -equipped 91st squadriglia. By November, when the 91st exchanged its SPAD S VIIs for the more potent SPAD S XIII, Baracca had taken his tally of 'kills' to 30. Some indication of how the German-led Austro-Hungarian thrust to the Piave was to effect the local air war can be gauged from the fact that over the next seven months, Major Baracca only managed to add a further 4 victories to his score, prior to meeting his own end, on 18 June 1918, when, having set off with two companions, he failed to return from a ground strafing mission. Italy's leading air ace, Baracca is seen here standing beside his SPAD XIII that carried his personal emblem of a rampant stallion. (Cowin Collection)

Below The sleek, diminutive **Nieuport 11 Bebe** provided the backbone of the Italian Military Air Services' fighter squadrons for around eighteen months prior to its being superseded by the SPAD S VII from mid-1917. Built under licence in Italy, by Nieuport-Macchi, the Italian machines carried their serial numbers on the fuselage, just aft and below the cockpit. The machine seen here carries the serial no Ni 3227. (Cowin Collection)

Below Alongside the 450 locally-built Nieuport 11s, Nieuport-Macchi also produced a follow-on batch of 150 **Nieuport 17s.** Seen here with its proud, young pilot is serial no Ni 3632. Note the command pennant that partially obscures the first letter of the aircraft's serial no. (Cowin Collection)

Opposite, top left The Italian Military Air Service relied totally on French developed fighters for its front-line equipment throughout the war. Interestingly, this photograph of an Italian operated **SPAD S VII** also includes a Nieuport 11, another of the French fighters the Italians favoured. However, unlike the Nieuport 11s and 17s that the Italian built under licence, all 197 Italian SPAD S VIIs were purchased directly from France. (Cowin Collection)

Below and above right An extremely revealing air-to-air photograph of the **Caproni Ca 33** four man bomber developed from the original twin-boom fuselaged Caproni Ca 30 of 1913. Initially completed towards the end of 1915, the Ca 33 made its operational debut during the latter half of 1916. One of the first large bombers to be fielded, the Ca 33 was powered by three 150hp Isotta-Fraschini V-4Bs that gave it a top level speed of 84mph at sea level. Capable of lifting a maximum bomb load of 1,000lb, the machine's range with this load was 280 miles. Although obscured by the upper wing in this view, the two tractor-propellered engines were mounted at the front of each fuselage boom, while the pusher-propellered engine formed the rear of the central nacelle. Besides the two, side-by-side pilots, the Ca 33 carried a front gunner and a rear gunner, just visible below, who stood in a curious, open pulpit-like framework directly above the rear engine. The ground view above of the Ca 33 is of interest in that it lacks the standard pulpit-mounted rear gunner's position completely. At least 250 Ca 33s were built, the type being operated by both the Italians and the French. (Cowin Collection)

Below Deliveries of the 300 **Savoia-Pomilio SP 3** two-seat reconnaissance machines might have been more understandable had they been made two or even three years earlier, as it was they started in mid-1917. Clearly, by this time, not even the powerful 300hp Fiat A 12Bis fitted could give this tired old pusher-engined design suffecient impetus to extricate it from hostile fighter attack. The resultant operational loss rate was high and SP 3 crew morale low. (Cowin Collection)

Above The **Caproni Ca 42**, powered by three 400hp Isotta-Fraschini, or Libertys, was the last and the heaviest of the Caproni triplane bombers to be produced. Delivered in early 1918, these five-man machines carried up to 3,910lb of bombs in a central housing attached to the lower wing. Top level speed of the Ca 42 was 87mph at 6,560 feet, while its defensive armament consisted of five Ravelli machine guns. Over 20 of these mammoth triplanes were built, the machine seen here carrying the British serial no N 527, being the second of six Ca 42s operated by the RNAS for a period during 1918. (Cowin Collection)

Below An admirable ground view of an Italian operated **Hanriot HD-1**, serial no Hd 13244, seen in a mid to late 1918 setting. Although slow by contemporary standards and with only a single .303-inch Vickers gun, distinctly underarmed, the Hanriot was both very agile and robust, features that clearly endeared it to the Italians to such an extent that they foresook the much faster SPAD S XIII in favour of this more nimble mount. Indeed, at the time of the Armistice in November 1918, Italy had bought no fewer than 831 of these machines, ensuring that no fewer than sixteen of the total eighteen existing Italian fighter squadrons were equipped with the Hanriot. (Cowin Collection)

Below While the four man, biplane **Caproni Ca 46** may have been the last of the company's illustrious line of World War I bombers, it was also the machine to be built in the greatest numbers by far, with 255 built in Italy by the parent company and sub-contractors, and more had been built in France by REP, plus five of the 1,000 ordered from Standard of the 400hp Liberty-engined version for use by American forces. Developed from the Ca 44 of early 1917, the Ca 46 was powered by three 300hp Fiat A 12s, giving it a top level speed of 95mph at 6,560 feet. Capable of carrying a bomb load of 1,300lb over a range of 760 miles, the machine had an operational ceiling of 15,000 feet (Cowin Collection)

first flew in late 1917, the type entering operational service by mid-1918. At the time of the Armistice, 57 of these handsome looking machines had been delivered. The M 8 was the last in a wartime series of small, pusher-engined naval flying boats produced by Macchi starting with the **Macchi L 1**, seen here in the smaller of the two images. This too had been a two seater, but was little more than a copy of an Austro-Hungarian Navy Lohner Type L that had fallen into Italian hands within a matter of days after Italy had entered the war. Before a month was out, Nieuport-Macchi, as it was then, had selected the 150hp Isotta-Fraschini to power their copy and by late 1915 were delivering the first of the total of 139 L 1s produced. (Cowin Collection)

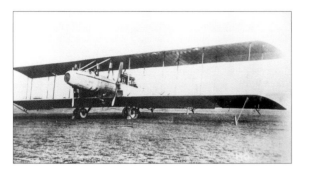

Below The two seat **Macchi M 8** maritime patrol aircraft was a scaled-up development of the single seat Macchi M 7 flying boat. Powered by a 160hp Isotta-Fraschini V-4B, the M8

The Yanks Are Coming!

To say that the aviation communities of the US Army and Navy were unprepared for war when their President took them into it on 6 April 1917 would be to understate the situation: in fact, preparations were virtually non-existent. In all, at this time, the US Army had less than 250 aeroplanes, while the Navy and its Marine Corps had 54 heavier-than-air machines, one small airship and three balloons. Spread throughout the continental US, Panama, Hawaii and further west across the Pacific, the threat that these mainly training assets

constituted hardly amounted to a hill of beans! What was worse was that very few serving US officers had much of an inkling of the kind of warfare being practised by the Europeans, who, pre-occupied as they were with the fighting, discouraged US military and naval observers from getting in their way. Happily, as it transpired there were a handful of Americans, those that had volunteered to fly and fight with the British, French and Italians, who had learnt hard-won lessons at first hand. Within the year, these men would become the youthful leaders of the

rapidly expanding US Army, Navy and Marine Corps aviation assets.

Washington DC was a fairly busy place in the weeks after America joined the war. Plans needed to be laid and for these many of hundreds of millions of Federal Government dollars had to be voted and allocated. Not just the Army and Navy were wrestling to secure their own cherished priorities, US industry had to be organised and set on a wartime footing. The task facing the politicians and planners alike was a formidable one. That some of this planning was to prove optimistic was only to be expected and this was very much the case with the initial military and naval aviation requirements and growth projections, but what America was to go on to produce once more realistic goals had been set was still

little short of miraculous, as a brief review of what the US aviation industry achieved goes to show.

Between the end of 1903 and 1916, the whole of the US aircraft industry had produced less than 1,000 aeroplanes, but, by June 1917 was being exhorted to produce 22,625 aeroplanes and 44,000 aero-engines, plus 80% spares of each within the following eighteen month period. The fiction of this War Department projection, admittedly by far the most unrealistic of all the initial plans, was discernible within the year.

However, even after being revised downwards, what the industry achieved was impressive enough. Take the example of the Dayton-Wright-built DH 4, production of which rose from 15 aircraft a month in April 1918 to 1,097 machines per month by October 1918. By the time of the Armistice, well over 3,000 DH 4s, plus 7,800 trainers had been produced, making a total of nearly 11,000 aircraft. This truly mammoth effort from such a still infant US industry should be compared to that of the far larger and mature (though obviously stretched) French industry. In a move to hedge their bets, the US Government had, in August 1917, placed orders for 5,875 aircraft, plus 8,500 aero-engines with French suppliers. By 1 July 1918, the French had only managed to delivery a quarter of the promised aircraft, with engine deliveries being even more dismal, resulting in the US cancelling their outstanding orders.

The other planning aspect of America's entry into the war that begs a brief review concerns the initial decision to 'buy in' existing French, British and Italian designs to produce, rather than to lose valuable production engineering time waiting for the US industry to develop its own designs. Even without the benefit of the historian's hindsight, this was clearly the best path to follow for such an embryo industry.

However, there was one glorious exception to this quite uncharacteristic American reticence to venture too deeply and quickly into the unknown, that exception being the Liberty aero-engine. Drawn up at the end of May 1917, as either an eight or twelve cylinder power unit, the first eight cylinder engine was delivered for testing just over a month later, on 4 July 1917, while the first twelve cylinder unit commenced flight testing on 21 October 1917. The flow of Liberty engines to America's European allies that commenced early in 1918 was of inestimable value in unclogging the long-standing bottleneck caused by the European's inability to produce aero-engines as fast as airframes.

For the purposes of continuity, the writer has chosen to include the first of America's own combat aircraft designs in this chapter, rather than in the following one dealing with 1918.

Left Both manpower and material were major initial contributions America brought to the war as pictured by these US Army Signal Corps mechanics re-assembling **Nieuport 17s** at Issoudun in France during May 1917. After August 1917, Issoudun was to become the biggest and best known of the sixteen American advanced flying training schools established in France. At the time of the Armistice, these flying training schools were producing around 2,000 pilots per month, including those undergoing refresher training. (US National Archives)

Below Despite having been born in France of French parentage, **Raoul Gervais Victor Lufbery** has deservedly gone into the annals of aviation as one of the brave young men who helped in the forging of US military aviation during World War I . Lufbery was born on 14 March 1885, emigrating with his parents to the US at the start of the 1890s. At seventeen and footloose, Lufbery ran away from home, travelling to Europe and the Middle East before returning to the US to join the Army as a rifleman. It was the US Army that furthered his knowledge of the world by sending him to the Philippines, from

where, on Army discharge, he proceeded to explore South East Asia in 1910. Two years on and Lufbery's path crosses that of French pilot, Marc Pourpe, who hired Lufbery as the mechanic for his Bleriot. At the outbreak of war both men were still together and, by now, back in France. Pourpe volunteered and with his previous flying experience soon found himself with Escadrille N 23. Initially rejected as a foreigner by the French authorities, Lufbery was contemplating joining the French Foreign Legion when Pourpe, in need of a tried and trusted mechanic, intervened on his behalf. Sadly, shortly after rejoining Pourpe, his benefactor was killed. During the late spring of 1915, Lufbery was selected for pilot training, gaining his 'wings' on 29 July 1915. His introduction to combat came in October 1915 piloting two seater Voisins with Escadrille VB 106. Happily for Lufbery, he was selected for single seaters early in 1916 and following type conversion training joined the Nieuport 11-equipped Escadrille Lafayette on 24 May 1916. French-led, this unit was manned by American volunteer pilots. Here, within the space of less than five months, Lufbery made his mark by becoming an ace, that is having amassed the necessary five 'kills', on 12 October 1916. Commissioned in early 1917, Lufbery continued flying for the French with the Escadrille Lafayette until January 1918, when the unit and its personnel were transferred to the American Expeditionary Forces's control. By now holding the US rank of major, Lufbery was given command of the 94th Aero, equipped with Nieuport 28s. This unit became operational on 19 March 1918 and two months later Raoul Lufbery was killed after falling from his blazing Nieuport on 19 May 1918. Seen here standing besides his Nieuport 11, with its Escadrille Lafayette's Indian Head emblem, Lufbery's ultimate confirmed score stood at 17 'kills'. (Cowin Collection)

Below A foursome of **Nieuport 17s** belonging to the **Escadrille Lafayette**, or N 124, formed of French command-ed American volunteer pilots. The brainchild of Norman Price, an American lawyer, the squadron came into being on 16 April 1916, as the Escadrille Americaine, its name being quickly changed to Lafayette following German diplomatic pressure. After serving honourably under the French flag for just under two years, the unit was transferred to US control on 18 February 1918 to become the 103rd Aero Squadron, with most of its pilots being put in command of other squadrons being formed at the time, thus helping to spread this pool of hard-won combat experience. Sadly, the squadron's creator, Norman

Price, along with other unit members including Raoul Lufbery, James McConnell and Kiffen Rockwell were all to die in combat. Note the squadron's Indian Head emblem (US National Archives)

Below During 1914, the Curtiss Company had produced a couple of two seater biplanes, known as their Model J and Model N. However, even before the year had ended, the company had merged the best features of the two machines to produce the **Curtiss JN**. Sales of what was to become the legendary JN started slowly, with an initial eight being bought by the US Army in December 1914, primarily for reconnaissance duties. The first large order for the machine came from Britain's RNAS, whose first order for 79 JN-3 trainers was placed in March 1915. This, of course, was only the start, with more than 7,500 examples of the JN in all its variants going on to be built. Seen here is RNAS JN-3, serial no 3376. The RNAS JN-3s used a 100hp Curtiss OXX-2, giving them a top level speed of 82mph at sea level. (Philip Jarrett Collection)

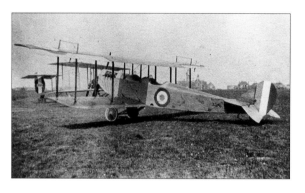

Below Designed as a tactical reconnaissance two seater, the **Curtiss R-2** first flew towards the close of 1915. Powered by a 160hp Curtiss V-X, the R-2 had a top level speed of 86mph at sea level, along with a useful endurance of up to 6 hours 40 minutes. Twelve of these machines were sold to the US Army, followed by an order for 100 from Britain's RFC, who replaced the Curtiss engines with 200hp Sunbeams. The US Army machine seen here was one of those deployed as part of the US punitive expedition sent to Mexico in 1916. (Cowin Collection)

Above The sole **Curtiss S-2 Wireless** single seat scout, seen here without its twin, broad-bladed propeller, along with the associated inner and outer spinners, the purpose of which was to funnel cooling air to the annular engine radiator revealed in this view. First flown in the summer of 1916 and demonstrated to the press by Curtiss pilot Victor Carlstrom on 9 August 1916, the S-2 was powered by a 100hp Curtiss and achieved a top level speed of 119mph at sea level. Despite its neat appearance, the S-2 was generally conceded to be around two years behind its European contemporaries, thanks to America's isolation from the design impetus provided by wartime developments. (Cowin Collection)

Above The **Thomas-Morse S-4C** was the nearest thing to a single seat fighter that America was to produce during World War I. The design of the S-4 was started in the autumn of 1916, ahead of the January 1917 founding of the Thomas-Morse Company that was to produce it. Initially powered by the troublesome 100hp US licence-built Gnome Monosoupape, later replaced by a 100hp Le Rhone C9, the first S-4 made its initial flight in the spring of 1917, leading to its evaluation by the US Army's McCook Field in June 1917. Satisfied by these trials, the Army ordered 100 modified machines with a shorter fuselage and smaller control surfaces, known as S-4Bs, for use as unarmed fighter trainers. Ordered in October 1917, the first of the S-4Bs were delivered the following month. In January 1918, the Army placed an initial order for 50 of the single .300-inch Marlin armed S-4Cs. In all, the Ithaca, New York-based company went on to build a known 609 S-4s, of which the S-4C was the dominant version. Even US Navy bought a known twelve. Although clearly obsolescent by 1918 standards, the underpowered and underarmed S-4C, with its 95mph top level speed was reported to have been quite agile, if a little tail-heavy. The US Army S-4C seen here, serial no 38635, was photographed at San Diego's Rockwell Field in late 1918 (Cowin Collection)

Below The **Curtiss R-6** of early 1917 was a two seat reconnaissance machines flown by both the US Navy and US Army, who ordered 76 and 18 examples, respectively. It should be noted that eight of the Army machines were transferred to the Navy prior to delivery. Powered by a 200hp Curtiss V-Z-3, the R-6, with its top level speed of 83mph was not a very vivid performer, being best remenmbered as being the first US aircraft to be operationally deployed overseas. This came about when the US Marines' 1st Aeronautical Company took its R-6s to Ponta Delgada in the Azores, on 21 January 1918. The machine seen here, Bu Aer A 193, is of interest in being the only R-6 to be fitted with a single, central float, plus outriggers, the rest of the R-6s using the conventional twin float arrangement. (Cowin Collection)

Below As mentioned in the introduction to this chapter, some aircraft types were bought directly from the French for use by the American Expeditionary Forces. One such aircraft being the fast, two seat **Breguet Bre14B** day bomber. The one seen here belonged to the 96th Aero Squadron, with its emblem comprising a red devil clutching a white bomb, all framed by a white triangle. Formed early in 1918, the 96th Aero was declared operational on 29 May 1918. (Cowin Collection)

Below **Edward Vernon Rickenbacker** was born in Columbus, Ohio, of poor Swiss immigrant parents, on 8 October 1890. 'Eddy', as he was almost universally known, had his education cut short at the age of twelve, when the death of his father forced him to become the family breadwinner. 'Eddy'

worked at a number of mundane jobs, until, at eighteen, he joined a car sales and service company. Here he rose rapidly from drip tray cleaner to racing driver. At the age of twenty, 'Eddy' Rickenbacker, driving a Blitzen-Benz, set a new land speed record of 134mph. A year on and he was driving in the first of the famed Indianappolis 500 races. When America entered the war in April 1917, 'Eddy' joined the US Army, becoming personal driver to General Pershing, the US Army commander in France. It was here that 'Eddy' met Brigadier General 'Billy' Mitchell. As a reward for repairing his Mercedes, Mitchell arranged for 'Eddy' to enter flying training at one of the US-operated French military flying schools in August 1917. Now a pilot and with a commission, he joined the newly formed 94th Aero Squadron on 4 March 1918. Flying Nieuport 28s at the time he joined it, as seen here, the unit was soon to exchange its Nieuports for SPAD S XIIIs. Rickenbacker's first confirmed 'kill' was when he downed a Pfalz D III on 29 April 1918. By the time of the Armistice, a little over six months later, Captain 'Eddy' was America's leading air ace with a confirmed 26 victories. After a series of business triumphs and tragedies during the 1920s, 'Eddy' Rickenbacker's fortunes steadied, with him becoming first General Manager, later Chairman of Eastern Air Lines. During a World War II tour of the Pacific area, 'Captain Eddy' had the misfortune to have to spend some days in a dinghy, prior to rescue, after the aircraft he was flying in was forced to crash land at sea. 'Eddy' Rickenbacker finally died of old age on 27 July 1973. (US Air Force)

the ability to reach 10,000 feet in 10 minutes 18 seconds. Armed with two .303-inch Vickers guns, the Ni 28 was fast and agile, but soon gained a dubious reputation for shedding upper wing leading edge fabric and, occasionally the whole upper wing, when dived too steeply. Although this problem had been remedied by July 1918, the Americans, like the French. had by then re-equipped with SPAD S XIIIs. In all the Americans ordered 297 Ni 28s. Seen here is one of the development machines with dihedral on the upper wings only and smaller than the definitive gap between top wing and fuselage. (US Air Force)

Above right First flown on 14 June 1917, the **Nieuport Ni 28** fighter abandoned the characteristic Nieuport 'V' interplane strut in favour of the conventional twin strut arrangement. It was during the somewhat protracted development of the Ni 28, that the French authorities elected to standardise on the SPAD S XIII. Meanwhile, Nieuport were clearly less than happy with the design, having to produce four versions of the machine prior to its initial deliveries with the American Expeditionary Forces' 27th, 94th, 95th and 147th Aero Squadrons in March 1918. Powered by a 160hp Gnome Monosoupape, the single seater had a top level speed of 123mph at 6,560 feet, along with

Below The **SPAD S XIII** of the 22nd Aero Squadron, seen here, was an early production example of 893 S XIIIs purchased by the American Expeditionary Force and used a 200hp Hispano-Suiza 8B, rather than the 235hp 8 Bec of later aircraft. Contracts for another 6,000 Curtiss-built machines were cancelled in the wake of the Armistice, but 435 existing S XIIIs were shipped back to the US after the war, being used as fighter trainers, following re-engining with the de-rated 180hp Wright-Hispano. Incidentally, the 22nd Aero was declared operational on 22 August 1918 and was one of the few units to survive the immediate post-war run-down to become the 22nd Pursuit Squadron. (US National Archives)

Above One of the beneficiaries of the American decision to build existing types, while 'home grown' products were being developed was the **Airco DH 4**, of which 4,846 were built in the US, primarily by Dayton-Wright. In October 1918 one of these machines became the DH 4B after its conversion to mimic the closer crew positions of the Airco DH 9. Using a 416hp Liberty 12A, the **DH 4B** had a top level speed of 124mph at sea level. By the time the conversion programme came to an end in 1923, another 1,537 DH 4s had become DH 4Bs. (US National Archives)

Opposite, top **Elliott White Springs**, son of a reasonably wealthy mill owner, was born in South Carolina on 31 July 1896. It was while White Springs was at Princeton University that America entered the war in April 1917. Filled with the patriotic zeal of youth, along with an initial introduction to aviation provided by Princeton, White Springs gained a commission

Above Observer Lt John H. Snyder of the 91st Aero Squadron hands down the photographic evidence gleaned during his latest mission for dispatch to the photographic laboratory. Based at Gondreville-sur-Moselle, the 91st Aero Squadron, equipped with **Salmson 2A 2s**, had a short, but lively five month operational existence, extending from 7 June 1918 to 11 November 1918. During this time the 91st Aero lost 13 fliers, along with another 13 wounded. Set against this, the 91st Aero was credited with downing no less than 21 enemy fighters. (US National Archives)

Right The men and machines of the 11th Aero Squadron, operational from 5 September 1918. The **DH 4s** carry the unit emblem on their noses. This consisted of a comic strip character called 'Jigs', who is toting a bomb under his right arm. (US National Archives)

promoted to Captain and given command of the 148th, now re-assigned to the US 4th Pursuit Group. Not happy with life back in the US after the war, White Springs returned to Paris, where he wrote a best seller 'War Birds', based on his experiences. Later and now more settled, White Springs returned to the US, taking the family business to new heights. Elliott White Springs, seen here standing beside his British marked Sopwith Camel, died on 15 October 1959. (US National Archives)

Below Any American career the **Handley Page 0/400** may have made for itself was to be overtaken by the Armistice, with only a handful of the 1,500 US machines ordered having been completed. Modified to take twin 400hp Liberty 12 Ns, these American 0/400s were built by the Standard Aircraft Corporation of Elizabeth, New Jersey. The Standard-built, Liberty-powered 0/400 seen here at Kelly Field, Texas, is flanked by a Thomas-Morse S-4 on the left and a Curtiss JN on the right. (US National Archives)

Below Designed by the US Navy's Jerome Hunsaker specifically as a submarine killer, the ungainly-looking **Navy Aircraft Factory N-1** was built to carry a nose-mounted Davis gun, a recoilless weapon firing 6lb shells. Work on this, the first of the Navy Aircraft Factory's designs, with its 360hp Liberty pusher-engine, started in February 1918, with the first of four making its maiden flight on 22 May 1918. The top level speed of this two seater was 94mph at sea level. The flight development phase of the N-1 was far from being the smoothest, with the first having both floats collapse on touch down from its first flight, with two others suffering severe damage shortly afterwards, leading to the N-1's abandonment. (US National Archives)

in the US Army and set sail for Britain and six months of flying training in September 1917. During his training, White Springs was fortunate enough to benefit from the tutelage of Canadian fighter ace 'Billy' Bishop. Clearly, White Springs, himself must have been an excellent pupil, for, later, when Bishop, as leader of the RAF's crack No 85 Squadron, was busy readying the unit for operations with their Royal Aircraft Factory SE 5a, he invited White Springs to join him. On 22 May 1918, No 85 Squadron crossed the English Channel and ten days later White Springs got his first confirmed 'kill' in the shape of a Pfalz D III. By 27 June 1918, the youthful American's score had risen to 4, at which time he was shot down and slightly wounded himself.. In July he was transferred, as a flight commander, to the all-American, Sopwith Camel-equipped 148th Aero Squadron attached to the British 65 Wing. Here, with the 148th Aero, between 3 August 1918 and 5 September 1918, White Springs was to add a further eight victories to his tally, bringing his final wartime total to 12. In October 1918 White Springs was

Above First flown on 5 July 1918, the **Curtiss 18T Wasp**, powered by the new 400hp Curtiss-Kirkham K-12, had been developed against a US Navy need for a two seat reconnaissance fighter. Despite proving to be tail-heavy during its maiden flight, necessitating the introduction of a five degree sweepback to its triplane wings, the 18T's speed and climb performance were little short of phenomenal. Capable of a top level speed of 163mph at sea level, coupled to an ability to reach 10,400 feet in 10 minutes, the 18T went on to set a new World Altitude record of 34,910 feet on 18 September 1919. While these figures would have been somewhat reduced in the case of the production aircraft, with its five .30-inch guns and other service equipment, there is still no doubt that this machine would have provided a headache for the German fighter defences had the war continued. As it was, only five examples of the 18T Wasp were built consisting of two for the US Navy, two for the US Army, along with a fifth civilian model, sold to Bolivia in 1919. The 18T seen here was Bu Aer A3325, the first of the two US Navy machines. (Curtiss)

Below Essentially an improved version of the Curtiss H-16, via the John Cyril Porte developed Felixstowe F 5, the first **Navy Aircraft Factory F-5-L** made its maiden flight in late July 1918. Powered by two 420hp Liberty 12As, the four man F-5-L carried six .303-inch Lewis guns for its defence, along with up to four 230lb bombs for more aggressive purposes. Top level speed of the F-5-L was 90mph at sea level, with a range of 830 miles being attainable at its economic cruise speed. Besides being responsible for the design's 'Americanisation' in terms of its production engineering, the Navy Aircraft Factory went on to produce 138 of these flying boats, of which 33 had been completed at the time of the Armistice, or just over three months after the F-5-L's first flight. Clearly considered a priority naval programme, 60 more F-5-Ls were built by Curtiss, while a further 30 were completed in Canada before post-war contract cancellations took effect. (US National Archives)

Opposite, top left and right **Chance Milton Vought**, the son of a prominent boatbuilder, was born in New York City on 26 February 1890. At the age of 20 and with a strong technical bias to his education, the impatient young Vought, who had already restyled himself Chance, from Chauncey, left college in 1910 to join an engineering firm in Chicago. It was during these early days in Chicago that Chance Vought was to be bitten by the 'aviation bug'. Vought learnt to fly on a Wright Model B of the Lillie Aviation Company, in which he is seen here, gaining FAI Licence No 156 on 14 August 1912. Despite having risen to head the Experimental Development Department of the company he had joined in 1910, Vought's love of things aeronautical lead him to join the Lillie Aviation School in 1913 as their maintenance engineer, ground school lecturer and instructor pilot. While here, Vought masterminded the conversion of a Wright Model B into the 1913 two seat Lillie-Vought

man, pilot and playboy, who shortly after the corporation's foundation, left for France as part of General Pershing's staff, only to be killed in a flying accident. Back in Long Island, Vought was busy creating his two seat VE-7 advanced trainer, the aircraft that established the Chance Vought name in the annals of 20th Century aviation. In 1922, the company became the Chance Vought Corporation, going on to produce the US Navy Corsair biplanes of the 1920s and '30s, the F4U Corsair fighter of World War II and the Mig-killing F8U Crusader carrier jet of 1957. Tragically, Chance Vought died of scepticaemia, still only 40 years of age, on 25 July 1930. The image above shows the first of the many **Lewis and Vought VE-7s** to be built. First flown in February 1918, this 150hp Hispano-Suiza A engined two seater had a top level speed of 106mph at sea level. Although too late to be useful for wartime pilot training with the US Army, who had taken eight of the envisaged 1,014 examples ordered at the end of the war, the VE-7 went on the become a major element of immediate post-war US naval aviation, with a total of 129 being used variously as trainers, armed two seat scouts and even single seat fighters, most versions having the option of fitting wheels or floats. (both Vought)

Above On 17 January 1918 Glenn L Martin received a US Army contract to design and produce ten examples of a twin-engined, four seat reconnaissance bomber. In the absence of any military lead, the aircraft was called the **GMB**, short for **Glenn Martin Bomber** and came together fairly quickly under the supervision of Martin's Young Chief Engineer, Donald W. Douglas. First flown on 15 August 1918, the GMB was powered by two 400hp Liberty 12As that gave the biplane atop level speed of 1015mph at sea level, dropping to 100mph at 6,500 feet. Armed with five .30-inch Marlin machine guns, the GMB could lift a 1,040lb bomb load over a range of 390 miles at a cruising speed of 92mph. With the first aircraft delivered to the US Army in October 1918, the company had delivered all but one by the time of the Armistice, the tenth machine being completed in 1919 as a passenger transport. (Glenn L. Martin)

Tractor. Once again, this work clearly did not stretch him sufficiently, with Vought moving on, in 1914, to become Editor of the weekly *Aero and Hydro* magazine. In parallel with his editorial duties, Vought got his first real design opportunity, when he drew up and supervised assembly of the two seat PLV biplane, first flown in August 1914. By now tiring of journalism, Vought joined the Curtiss Aeroplane Company in the summer of 1915, having spent some of his early 1915 months drawing up the plans and supervising the building of the Mayo-Vought-Simplex two seat trainer, first flown in May 1915. In the autumn of 1915, the footloose Vought moved from Curtiss to join the Wright Company as Chief Engineer. Vought retained this job title after Orville Wright and Glenn Martin came together to form the relatively short-lived, but prestigious-sounding Wright-Martin Company in August 1916. Wright-Martin then acquired the Simplex Motor Car Company and the Mayo Radiator Works, producers of the earlier Mayo-Vought-Simplex machine. This provided Vought with the opportunity to develop his earlier 90hp Mayo design into the sole 150hp Wright-Martin Model V two seater, first flown in September 1916. An admirable enough aircraft in itself, the Model V was to flounder in a morass of Franco-American politics and corporate skulduggery, that involved the non-delivery of 700 licence-built Hispano engines to France and brought about the breakup of the Wright-Martin enterprise. However, happily for Chance Vought, before the Wright-Martin breakup occurred, the company had sent him to Europe for five months, where he had an opportunity to inspect the latest European design practices at first hand. Thus, when America entered the war in April 1917, the 27 year old Vought, intent on forming his own company, went looking for a partner with money and the contacts to complement his technical expertise. Thus, on 18 June 1917, was formed the Lewis and Vought Corporation, with Chance M. Vought as Chairman and President. Incidentally, the Lewis in the company's title, referred to Birdseye B. Lewis, an independently wealthy sports-

1918

There is an old naval dictum to the effect that the victor in any surface action is likely to be the one who has the greatest numbers of hulls in the water. While some armchair strategists might object to it, arguing that it ignores or places any inequities in quality below that of pure quantity, the adage has the irritating trait of proving to be mostly right for the many centuries of recorded naval history. Certainly, this issue of quantity overwhelming quality seems to apply to way the war in the air evolved during 1918, as the ongoing erosion of the German aerial efforts showed. The Germans may well have shot down more Allied aircraft during 1918 than during previous years, but then, there were far more around to be shot down. Remember also the fact that

these Allied aircraft were capable of firing back and downing their quota of Germans and the whole matter resolves itself into a simple question of attrition, which, once the Americans had joined in, could not go in other than the Allies' favour.

This said, 1918 presents some fascinating questions and opportunities for the 'What if?' game. For example, it is pertinent to wonder just how much longer it would have taken the French and British builders to adopt the faster, more effective American production engineering practices, particularly when it came to aero-engine manufacture. Aero-engines have been chosen quite specifically, as, thanks to the level of effort and skill required, it was always going to take longer to produce an engine than

an airframe, with this disparity growing as the aircraft gets larger, needing multi-engines to get it into the air. Mention has already been made of the major contribution the US made to the outcome of the war in the air by its development and supply of the 400hp Liberty engine. What of other aero-engine developments of the time? Were, for instance, the British authorities to be accused of lacking resolve in not pushing the development of the air-cooled radial engine? Certainly, the failure of the ABC Wasp and its bigger brother the Dragonfly brought a premature end to a number of promising British combat aircraft and yet, by 1920, with little or nothing of the former wartime development funding available, Roy Fedden had produced and flown the first of the 400hp Bristol Jupiters. Interestingly, in France, the aero-engine development scene was, if anything, even more dismal than in Britain, with virtually all the focus being placed on the quite pedestrian development of mainly existing liquid-cooled, in-line engines.

Perhaps, after all, it was just as well that the 'hulls in the water' principle did hold true in this case, with Allied air power ultimately winning by sheer numbers.

Below First flown in May 1918, the giant **Handley Page V/1500**, along with the Bristol Braemar and Tarrant Tabor, had all been designed to carry a 1,000lb or more bomb load to Berlin from their No 27 Group, RAF, bomber bases in eastern England. Over a much shorter range, the V/1500 could carry a maximum bomb load of 7,500lb. The two machines seen here belong to No 166 Squadron, RAF, based at Bircham Newton, Norfolk. Deliveries of these aircraft had commenced in September 1918, only three having arrived at the time of the Armistice. (Ministry of Defence PRB/Crown Copyright)

Above By now screamingly anachronistic in its form, the **Voisin Type 10** two seat night bomber started to enter operational service in April 1918. Powered by a 300hp Renault, the Type 10 could carry up to 600lb of bombs and ammunition. With a top level speed of 82mph at sea level and a cruising speed of 76mph, the Type 10's endurance at cruising speed was four hours. Note how little the appearance of this, the culmination of a series of Voisins, had changed over the four years of war. (Cowin Collection)

Above The sole example of the single seat **Sopwith Type B 1 Bomber**, serial no B 1496, photographed in January 1918, while still at the manufacturers. Similar to the company's Cuckoo, but with two, rather than three bay interstrutted wings and a lighter looking landing gear, the B 1 was evaluated by the RNAS early in 1918. Subsequently being put into service with the Airco DH 4-equipped No 5 Wing, RNAS, based just outside Dunkirk, the B 1 was powered by a 200hp Hispano-Suiza, giving it a top speed of 118.5mph at 10,000 feet. The time to reach this altitude with a 560lb bomb load was cited as being 15 minutes 30 seconds. (Hawker)

Above and opposite, top Another story of an extremely useful fighter denied the Allies was that of the **Martinsyde F 4 Buzzard**, itself the last and by far most successful of a line of fighter designs that started with the two seat F 1 of early 1917. Counted among the fastest aircraft extant, the F 4 was powered by a 300hp Hispano-Suiza 8 Fb that endowed it with a top level speed of 140mph at sea level, decreasing to 132mph at 15,000 feet. Furthermore, the F 4's ability to reach 10,000 feet in 7 minutes 55 seconds represented a marked improvement over that of the Sopwith Snipe. The F 4's armament fit consisted of two synchronised .303-inch Vickers guns. First flown in early 1918, the F 4 was ordered into quantity production, but hold-ups with engine deliveries meant that only 48 F 4s had been handed over out of the 1,450 British orders at the time of the Armistice. Interestingly, in a reversal of the historic practice, this British fighter had been chosen for use by the

French, as it was by the Americans, but orders from these nations were cancelled at war end. Seen here in the larger image above is F 4, serial no D4263, while the smaller view is of serial no D 4256. (British Official/Crown Copyright)

first of the three examples on which work had commenced was to be completed and flown. It is seen here at Farnborough in mid-June 1918, following its Martlesham Heath trials of March 1918. (RAE/Crown Copyright)

Below If nothing else this trim-looking triplane helps illustrate the point that for every winning design, a number of other design submissions fall by the wayside. First flown in February 1918, the company-funded **Austin AFT 3 Osprey** was designed to meet the same Air Board's Type A 1(a) requirement that led to the production contract for Sopwith's Snipe. Powered by a 230hp Bentley BR 2, the Osprey's top level speed was 118.5mph at 10,000 feet, this height being reached in 10 minutes 20 seconds. Armament consisted of three forward-firing .303-inch guns, of which two were fixed and synchronised Vickers, backed by an overwing Lewis that could be swivelled in elevation for 'belly-raking' an adversary's underside. Only the

Above The **Supermarine N 1B Baby** may not have been the world's first single seat flying boat fighter, but it can lay claim to being the first of British design. First flown in February 1918, two N 1Bs were to be built to meet an Admiralty requirement, the first, serial no N59, being powered by a 200hp Hispano-Suiza, while N60 used the 200hp Sunbeam Arab. Top level speed attained by N 1B, N59, was 117mph at sea level. The Admiralty decision to operate Sopwith Pup and Camel fighters from aboard ship eliminated the need for such as the N 1B, but Supermarine managed to incorporate much of this basic design into their Sea Lion I and II, the latter winning the 1922 Schneider Trophy after the previous year's event had been aborted. (Vickers)

Above and right Another example of an opportunity frittered away, the **Airco DH 10** Amiens could well have played a useful role on the Allies' behalf, had not nearly eighteen months been lost to policy vacillation. A simple development of the Airco DH 3 of early 1916, the first of four prototype Airco DH 10 Amiens made its maiden flight on 4 March 1918 and proved under-powered on the output of its two 230hp Siddeley Pumas mounted as pushers. The second prototype, serial no C 8659 seen here in the larger image above, used twin, tractor-mounted 375hp Rolls-Royce Eagle VIIIs, while the third prototype had two 400hp Liberty 12s, again tractor-mounted. It was this

machine that served as the standard for subsequent production Amiens. Essentially too late to play any real part in the air war, this three man bomber, with its top level speed of 117.5mph at 6,500 feet and maximum1,380lb bomb load was just entering large-scale production at the time of the Armistice. Of the 1,295 DH 10 and DH 10a Amiens ordered, only eight were in the RAF's hands, of which two examples had been delivered to No 104 Squadron, RAF, at Azelot at war end. However, some of the 268 DH 10s built did enter post-war service with Nos 60. 97. 120 and 216 Squadrons, RAF. The smaller of the two images show a production DH 10C Amiens III, serial no E5557. (both de Havilland)

Opposite, bottom If nothing else, the **Felixstowe F 5** should have served to highlight some of the shortfalls in British production engineering practice compared with that of the Americans. The prototype of this large maritime patrol aircraft had first flown in April 1918. However, the first production F 5 did not emerge until a year later, differing in considerable detail from the prototype. Compare this with the progress recorded in the previous chapter on the Americanised version of the F 5, the Navy Aircraft Factory F-5-L that first flew in late July 1918 and yet 33 of which had been delivered by the time of the November 1918 Armistice. Powered by two 325hp Rolls-Royce Eagle VIIs, or 375hp Eagle VIIIs, the F 5's top level speed was 88mph at 2,000 feet. Seen here is serial no N 4637, the eighth of a 50 aircraft batch of F 5s built by Gosport Aviation Company. (Cowin Collection)

Below Another single seat fighter design of late 1917 origin doomed by using the ultimately abandoned 170hp ABC Wasp was the **Sopwith 8F1 Snail**. Of the six Snails ordered only two were to be completed, the first, serial no C 4284, with its fabric-on-stringer fuselage differing considerably from the second aircraft, serial no C 4288, seen here, with its monocoque plywood fuselage and forward staggered wings. To be armed with twin forward-firing, fixed and synchronised Vickers Guns, the Snail's performance, even without the engine troubles, appears to have been little better than that of the Sopwith Camel, leading to the Snail's abandonment. (Hawker)

Above The **Sopwith TF 2 Salamander** was an armour-clad version of the Sopwith Snipe used for close air support, or trench strafing duties. The first of three prototypes, serial no E5429 seen here, initially flew on 27 April 1918. Using the same engine and armament as the Snipe, the major difference between the two aircraft was the Salamander's additional 492lb of armour to protect the pilot. The Salamander's top level speed was 125mph at 3,000 feet, but the extra weight depressed the climb rate to a mediocre 6 minutes 30 seconds to reach 5,000 feet. (Hawker)

Above and left The giant **Handley Page V/1500**, successor to the the company's 0/100 and 0/400 bomber series, was another of those machines that arrived too late to effect the course of the air war. Initially, the V/1500 had been designed around two 600hp Rolls-Royce Condors, but development delays with this engine saw its substitution by four 375hp Eagle VIIIs. First flown on 22 May 1918, by Capt V.E.G. Busby from RAF Martlesham Heath, the original tail unit seen here in the ground view of prototype, serial no B 9463, proved unsatisfactory, being replaced by one with a much higher gap that raised the upper tailplane considerably. Capable of carrying a maximum bomb load of 7,500lb over short ranges, or 1,200lb to Berlin from its Norfolk base, the four man V/1500 had a top level speed of 97mph at 8,750 feet, along with an economic cruising speed of 90.5mph at 6,000 feet. At the time of the Armistice only three of the 255 V/1500s on order had been delivered to No 166 Squadron, RAF, at their Bircham Newton airfield, the rest being cancelled. The in-flight view is of a production V/1500 with the revised tail unit (Handley Page and Air Ministry PRB/Crown Copyright)

Opposite, top This **BAT FK 23 Bantam**, serial no F 1655, the third of nine production aircraft completed, proclaims its British Aerial Transport parentage in bold white lettering down its fuselage in place of the normal roundel, indicating that this photograph dates from after the war and that this was one of the machines sold as war surplus in 1919. The history of the Bantam is convoluted and starts in mid-1917 when Frederick Koolhoven left Armstrong Whitworth to join the newly formed Willesden-based BAT, taking his tell-tale FK design numbers with him. At BAT Koolhoven's first task centred on designing a

company-funded single seat fighter venture, designated FK 22. First flown in the early autumn of 1917 this machine gained Air Board interest and a contract for six examples followed. Originally planned to use a 120hp ABC Mosquito radial, one of the four FK 22s known to have been built and flown during 1918 used a 100 hp Gnome Monosoupape, subsequently replaced by a110hp Le Rhone 9J rotary. To compound matters, virtually all of the FK 22s varied in airframe detail, but out of this melée emerged the 170hp ABC Wasp powered example in the spring of 1918, the change being considered great enough to warrant the new designation of FK 23 Bantam. Others of the original FK 22 were re-engined with the Wasp, but all of these machines were criticised for the ease with which they would enter a vicious, flat or autorotative spin. To cure this problem, the later nine so-called production aircraft incorporated a modified set of increased span wings and tail unit. The later FK 23s that initially appeared in October 1918 had the by now standard twin Vickers guns, along with a top level speed of 128mph at 6,500 feet, falling to 118mph at 18,000 feet. Time to reach 10,000 feet took 9 minutes. Time, however, was about to run out on the Bantam with the coming of the Armistice. (British Aerial Transport)

Below Developed to meet the RAF's Type 1 Specification for a 180hp engined, single seat fighter replacement for the Sopwith

Camel, the attractively proportioned **Westland Wagtail** appears to have been a sound enough airframe design, let down by a totally undeveloped engine in the shape of the 170hp ABC Wasp. First flown during April 1918, the twin Vickers gunned Wagtail, like its its rivals, the BAT FK 23 Bantam and Sopwith Snail, was quietly left to wither away, following the official abandonment of the Wasp towards the close of 1918. Top level speed of the Wagtail was a useful 125mph at 10,000 feet, while it took a mere 3 minutes 30 seconds to reach an altitude of 5,000 feet. Interestingly, both of these performance figures are superior to those of the Sopwith Snipe with its far more powerful 230hp rotary. Only three Wagtails were to be completed, the last, serial no C 4293 being seen here. (Westland)

Above First flown at the end of May 1918, three of these **Blackburn Blackburd** single seat, torpedo bombers were built. Powered by a 375hp Rolls-Royce Eagle VIII, the machine's top level speed without and with torpedo was 95mph and 90.5mph at sea level, respectively. Later, slower and requiring more power than the existing Sopwith Cuckoo, development of the Blackburd did not proceed beyond the flight trial phase. Seen here is the ill-fated first aircraft, serial no N 113, that crashed during testing at Martlesham Heath at the beginning of July 1918. (Blackburn)

Below The company-funded, single seat **Sopwith Scooter** was the company's very first monoplane, the aircraft making its debut in June 1918. Purportedly built as an unarmed interim prototype for the Sopwith Swallow fighter, the Scooter actually served as Sopwith Test Pilot, Harry Hawker's personal aircraft. Powered by a 130hp Clerget, the Scooter used a Sopwith Camel fuselage. The sole Scooter never wore a military serial, its first identity being the civil K 135 seen here, later changed to G-EACZ. (Hawker)

Below Despite the fact that it emerged far too late to see combat during the war, the **Nieuport Ni 29** is of more than passing interest in that it serves to show the French trend towards heavier, more powerful fighters that was fully estab-

lished by the beginning of 1918. Flown initially in June 1918, the Ni 29 was a big, heavy, two-bay winged biplane that relied on the installed power of its 300hp Hispano-Suiza 8Fb for its performance, rather than its aerodynamics. Despite such criticism, this somewhat inelegant machine had a top level speed of 143mph at sea level, exactly comparable to Germany's best in the shape of the Junkers D I, while the Ni 29's ability to reach 16,405 feet in 14 minutes beat Germany's best climbing fighters, the Siemens-Schuckert D III and D IV.

Opposite, top H 5892 seen here, along with H 5893 were the only two **Sopwith Buffalo** two seat, close air support and reconnaissance machines built. As with the single seat Sopwith Salamander dealt with earlier, the Buffalo carried armour cladding to protect its crew from ground fire. In the case of the Buffalo, this armour plating covered the entire forward fuselage to a point just aft of the rear cockpit. Powered by a 230hp Bentley BR 2, the Buffalo had a top level speed of 114mph at 1,000 feet, while the machine took a laboured 4 minutes 55 seconds to reach 3,000 feet. First appearing in September 1918, the Buffalo appears to have been meagrely armed for a ground attack aircraft, carrying as it did a single, fixed, synchronised Vickers for the pilot, plus the observer's flexibly-mounted Lewis gun. Despite these apparent shortfalls, the Buffalo, according to the noted World War 1 aviation historian, Jack Bruce, was about to be ordered into production at the time of the Armistice. (Hawker)

Below Although not pursued beyond the prototype phase, the 1918 **BAT FK 24** Baboon two seat trainer, built to an Air Board requirement, is of interest in terms of its choice of engine, along with aspects of its structure. Its power came from the specified 170hp ABC Wasp I radial, an indication, albeit later shown to be ill-judged, of the faith officialdom placed in the ABC radials. The Baboon's structure was not just robust, it was deliberately designed to use as many interchangeable components as possible, including the ability to switch upper with lower wings, plus being able to swap port and starboard elevators with the rudder. The machine's extra wide wheel track is also notable. Top level speed of the Baboon was 90mph at sea level, while climb to 10,000 feet could be achieved in 12 minutes. Seen here is serial no D 9731, the first of six ordered and the only one believed to have been completed. (British Aerial Transport)

Below The sole **Sopwith Swallow**, serial no B 9276, photographed in October 1918. Employing a standard Camel fuselage, whose serial it used, the parasol-mounted wings had already been flown and tested on the Sopwith Scooter, dealt with above. Armed with twin, synchronised Vickers guns, the 110hp Clerget-engined Swallow had a top level speed of 113.5mph at 10,000 feet, some 7.5mph slower than the company's Snipe that was already in large scale production. (Hawker)

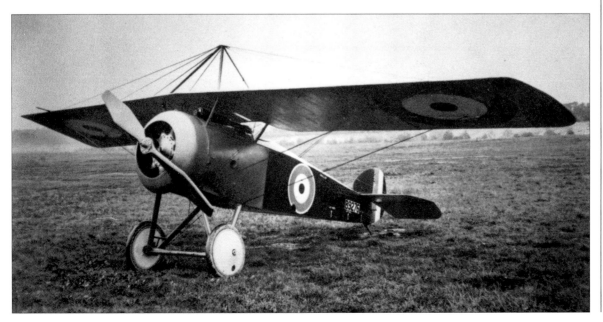

Index

INDEX TO AIRCRAFT

Airco DH 1 and 1A   35
Airco DH 2   36, 37
Airco DH 3A   39
Airco DH 4 and 4B   42, 82
Airco DH 5   44
Airco DH 6   46, 47
Airco DH 9 and 9A   28, 29, 48, 49
Airco DH 10
  Amiens   90
Alcock A 1   67
Armstrong
  Whitworth FK 8   40
Austin AFT 3
  Osprey   89
Avro 503 Type H   13
Avro 504   13
Avro 504B   55
Avro 504K   38, 39

BAT FK 23 Bantam   92, 93
BAT FK 24 Baboon   95
Bayard 'Fleurus'   10
Blackburn Blackburd   93
Blackburn GP
  and SP   62, 63
Blackburn Kangaroo   63
Blackburn TB   57
Bleriot XI - 2   16
Borel Monoplane   8, 9
Breguet Br 14A,
  B and H   26, 27, 80
Breguet-Michelin
  BM IV   21
Bristol F2A and B   41
Bristol M 1C   42
Bristol Scout
  C and D   32
Bristol S 2A   40

C Class Non-Rigid
  Airship   58
Caproni Ca 33   73
Caproni Ca 42   74
Caproni Ca 46   75
Caudron G III   16, 17
Caudron G IV   23
Caudron G VI   26
Curtiss 18T Wasp   84
Curtiss JN series   79
Curtiss R-2   79
Curtiss R-6   80
Curtiss S-2
  Wireless   79

De Havilland
  -see Airco
Dorand AR 1   23

Fairey Campania   63

Fairey Hamble Baby   64
Farman F 40   16
Farman HF 22   16
Felixstowe F 5   90, 91

Handley Page
  0/100   58
Handley Page
  0/400   58, 59, 83
Handley Page
  V/1500   86, 87, 92
Harriot HD-1   24, 74

Lewis & Vought VE-7   85

Macchi L 1   75
Macchi M 8   75
Martin GMB   85
Martinsyde F 4
  Buzzard   88, 89
Martinsyde G 100   37
Martinsyde S 1   32
Morane-Saulnier
  Type BB   57
  Type L   10, 57
  Type M   10
  Type N   18
  Type P   20

Navy Aircraft
  Factory
  F-5-L   84
Navy Aircraft
  Factory
  N-1   83
Nieuport Ni 10   56
Nieuport Ni 11
  Bebe   20, 68, 69, 72
Nieuport Ni 12   15
Nieuport Ni 16   21
Nieuport Ni 17   22, 72, 76, 77, 78
Nieuport Ni 23   23
Nieuport Ni 28   81
Nieuport Ni 29   94
Norman Thompson
  NT 2B   63

R 23 and R 23X
  Class Airship   65
Royal Aircraft Factory
  BE 2a and 2c   10, 30
  BS 1   11
  FE 2 series   33, 34
  FE 8   37
  FE 9   47
  RE 7   33
  RE 8   33
  SE 2   11
  SE 4   13
  SE 5 and 5a   5, 44, 45

Salmson 2A2   26, 82
Salmson Moineau   21
Savoia-Pomilio SP 3   73
Short Type 184   62
Short Type 310   62
Sikorsky Ilya
  Mourometz   70
Sikorsky S-20   71
SPAD S VII   24, 72, 73
SPAD S XIII   25, 81
Sopwith 3 Seat
  Tractor   12
Sopwith Type 9700
  1½ Strutter   21, 39, 52, 53, 59
Sopwith Anzani
  seaplane   12
Sopwith B 1   88
Sopwith Baby   56
Sopwith Bee   47
Sopwith Buffalo   94, 95
Sopwith 1F Camel   46
Sopwith 2F Camel   65, 66, 67
Sopwith Churchill   13
Sopwith T 1
  Cuckoo 1   64
Sopwith 5F Dolphin   48
Sopwith Type 9901
  Pup   7, 60
Sopwith 7F2
  Salamander   91
Sopwith Schneider   56
Sopwith Scooter   94
Sopwith 8F Snail   91
Sopwith 7F1 Snipe   50, 51
Sopwith Sparrow   49
Sopwith Swallow   95
Sopwith Tabloid   54, 55, 56
Sopwith Trainer   13
Sopwith Triplane   61, 62
Sopwith Type 807   55
Supermarine N 1B
  Baby   89

Thomas Morse S-4
  series   79

Vickers FB 5
  'Gun Bus'   32
Vickers FB 9   39
Vickers FB 12C   40, 41
Vickers FB14   40
Vickers FB 19 Mk II   47
Vickers FB 27 Vimy   51
Voisin LA Type III   18, 71
Voisin LB Type IV   18
Voisn Type 10   88
Vought - see Lewis
  & Vought

Westland N 1B   67
Westland Wagtail   93
Wight Quadruplane   63

INDEX TO PERSONALITIES

Ball, Albert, Capt, VC   30, 31
Baracca, Francesco,
  Major   71, 72
Barker, William,
  Major, VC   50, 51
Bishop, William,
  Major, VC   38
Collishaw, Raymond,
  Sdn Ldr   61
de Havilland, Geoffrey,
  Capt (later Sir)   42, 43
Dorme, Rene. Sous Lt   22
Fonk, Rene Paul,
  Capt, L d'H   25
Guynemer, Georges,
  L d'H   19
Hawker, Harry George   60
Hawker, Lanoe
  George, Major, VC   36
Lufbery, Raoul, Major   78
Mannock, Edward,
  Major, VC   44
McCudden, James,
  Major, VC   34, 35
Navarre, Jean, Sous Lt   17
Nungesser, Charles,
  Sous Lt   18, 19
Rhys-Davids, Arthur, Lt   45, 46
Rickenbacker, Edward
  Vernon. Capt   80, 81
Roe, Edwin Alliot
  Verdon (later Sir)   12
Rogers, William
  Wendell, Capt   51
Samson, Charles
  Rumney, Lt Col   54
Seversky de, Alexander,
  Major   70, 71
Sopwith, Thomas
  Octave Murdoch
  (later Sir)   11
Vought, Chauncey/
  Chance Milton   84, 85
Warneford, Reginald
  Alexander John,
  Flt Sub Lt, VC   57
White Springs, Elliott,
  Capt   82, 85